INTEGRATION TECHNOLOGY FOR CASE

Integration Technology for CASE

UNICOM

Applied Information Technology

edited by

Richard Daley

Avebury Technical

Aldershot · Brookfield USA · Hong Kong· Singapore · Sydney

Published by
Avebury Technical
Ashgate Publishing Limited
Gower House
Croft Road
Aldershot
Hants GU11 3HR
England

Ashgate Publishing Company
Old Post Road
Brookfield
Vermont 05036
USA

British Library Cataloguing in Publication Data

Integration Technology for CASE -
(UNICOM Applied Information Technology Series)
I. Daley, Richard II. Series
005.369

ISBN 0 291 39797 2

Printed and Bound in Great Britain by
Athenaeum Press Ltd, Newcastle upon Tyne.

Contents

Preface

This book contains papers from a seminar on Integration Technology for CASE plus invited papers. Although the seminar was directed at CASE the issues of integration go far beyond those needed for CASE alone and much of the technology described within this book has a much wider application within software-based systems.

The seminar and subsequently this book came about due to the growth in software engineering tools and environments and the overriding question of how do we get a group of disparate tools to work in unison. All the major hardware vendors have developed software engineering environments of one form or another into which, they expect, software tools from independent software vendors to be inserted. At the same time many users of software tools have found themselves attempting to put together a process of software development based upon the tools from the same independent software vendors.

The book consists of three parts. Part one introduces the topic of integration, concerning itself with the different facets of integration, the need for integration and the future direction that CASE integration must consider for successful adoption by industry at large.

Part two looks at the backbone of integration. Underlying the progress made on integration has been considerable work on initiatives and standards to support integration. The papers in part two provide an insight into the various standards, compares the standards and initiatives influencing the interchange and sharing of data by software tools, and, lastly, looks at the provision of a data exchange tool to support the interchange of data between different software tools, particularly when going from Upper CASE (i.e. analysis and design tools) to Lower CASE (i.e. implementation and construction tools, such as 4GLs).

In Part Three we concern ourselves with the development of CASE Frameworks which have pushed the frontiers of integration forward and provided, in many cases, commercial experience of integration standards. Through these papers we obtain vital evidence of the real-life experiences of users of CASE Frameworks.

Richard Daley
Richard Daley Associates

Abstracts

Integration Technologies available

The paper provides an introduction and overview to integration technologies currently available for CASE. It considers the underlying problems and issues of integration including data, control and presentation integration, and how these are supported by the current technologies. It concludes with an overview of the CASE Frameworks products available.

Integration. Why bother?

Many of us have experienced trying to integrate software and hardware from different vendors. And most of us have suffered in the process. Now we are being asked to go through all this pain again to integrate our development environment. Why bother? Is this the real way forward or more industry hype?

This paper examines the case for CASE integration. Firstly what we mean by integration, then why, when and how to go about it — and when not to. It describes where the benefits are today and where to expect them in the future.

The future direction for Integration Technology

In the paper various thoughts are presented about how the future for Integration Technology can be made more effective, easier to apply and use by simplifying the process of tool integration. The role of System Integrators is seen as vital to evolution in the application of Integration Technology.

Selected standardisation activities influencing CASE integration

There are numerous initiatives influencing the standards-making process with regard to CASE integration. The paper presents an overview of these activities including their heritage which is vital to gaining an insight into the complex process of standards selection and creation.

Data interchange between CASE tools: PCTE, IRDS or CDIF?

Three mechanisms which provide support for interchanging data between CASE tools are evaluated from various perspectives in the paper. The paper considers the reasons under which data interchange may be needed and how beneficial the different solutions are to supporting this interchange.

The underlying models used by the different data interchange mechanisms are investigated in conjunction with the complexities of data interchange. In its conclusions it identifies actions that a CASE user should consider if needing to interchange data and also actions for the CASE tool vendor.

Providing generic CASE integration

Migration and the sharing of data between CASE tools is the greatest barrier to effective CASE in the commercial environment. The paper describes the approach taken to providing a generic rules-based mechanism to support the integration of data between Upper CASE tools, data dictionaries and Lower CASE tools using a data exchange tool, EXCHANGE. It explains how companies are starting to prepare for using a shared data repository.

The Atherton Software BackPlane

The paper explains the approach taken by the Software BackPlane, namely to integrate existing tools from customers, implementing the actual processes in use and enforcing the workflow definition chosen by the customer. In addition the architecture of the Software Backplane, using an object-oriented repository is described.

ATIS (A Tool Integration Standard) is reviewed along with consideration of how the Software Backplane architecture will be influenced by developments such as ATIS, PCTE (Portable Common Tools Environment), Message-based architectures like BMS (Broadcast Message Services) and File-based architectures.

The Columbus SDE – an overview

The Columbus project of the European Space Agency (ESA) is one of Europe's largest projects involving several hundred software engineers throughout Europe. The paper presents an overview of the Columbus Software Development Environment (SDE) based on chosen tools for each life-cycle phase, the integration issues involved, and other considerations in delivering a turnkey SDE such as the responsibility for procurement, installation, training and maintenance.

Open IPSE with full life-cycle traceability

Underlying the Columbus SDE described in the preceding paper is a more generalised object-oriented IPSE. This paper provides an insight into this development particularly the ability to provide traceability throughout the life cycle. The notion of large-grain and fine-grain objects is introduced and how this influences the design of the IPSE by providing dual repository. Other capabilities of the IPSE to support integration are discussed, including the support for process integration through the definition of projects, user roles and access rights.

Digital's aerospace and defence software engineering environment

The paper describes the basic elements of Digital's COHESION approach to software development and in particular studies a specific use of COHESION to provide a software development environment for aerospace and defence (ASD/SEE).

The architecture of COHESION is explained along with how integration services are offered to allow third party tools to be incorporated into the environment. The current state of ASD/SEE is presented, including the integration issues involved, and how these will influence the evolution of the environment.

Entreprise II: the software engineering integrator

Entreprise II is a development environment for large software systems development. The paper presents the architecture of Entreprise II which is built upon and uses the services of PCTE (Portable Common Tools Environment). The integration services of Entreprise II are explained, including those for controlling data access, version control and the user interface.

Entreprise II offers a number of tools to support activities which extend across the software life cycle. These include documentation management, configuration management, traceability and project management, all of which are explained within the paper.

Part One

Integration Issues and Directions

1 Integration Technologies Available

Richard Daley
Richard Daley Associates

1 INTRODUCTION

Software Engineering is a complex business, possibly one of the most challenging engineering activities with which we are faced. It is undeniably a young discipline with a strong emphasis on craft as against engineering. Much of what we do is innovative rather than routine. To shift the emphasis we need to identify ways in which we can move activities from being innovative to being routine – or at least reduce the activity from 90 per cent creative to 90 per cent routine.

One way is through the use of software tools which assist us in automating the mundane aspects of the software development process whilst supporting the creative side of the job. The role of software tools and the importance of the software development process has received much attention of late, particularly as a result of the work of the Software Engineering Institute at Carnegie Mellon University in the USA. They have established an assessment programme used to determine the maturity of the software process within an organisation.

There are many software tools available from the suppliers of the computer hardware, from software vendors and, in some organisations, those produced locally for internal use. In fact the number of tools which may be of benefit on a specific project is overwhelming, with estimates of over 1500 tools being available. The issues faced are not those of not having the tools, instead they are how do we get to use the tools in a consistent and applicable fashion.

A survey that I conducted within a small community of CASE users who all used the same analysis and design tool identified a wide range of expectations in Tool Integration, particularly with the types of tools they wished to integrate within their Software Development Environments. Although a small sample, they identified twenty-three different software engineering areas in which they wanted to see support for integration, ranging from project management to the inspection process. In the same survey eighteen separate tools were identified which the respondents wished to see integrated. Not surprisingly many of these tools served the same functional areas.

One further reason for supporting integration relates to the lifetime of tools versus the lifetime of projects. It is quite common for projects to outlive the lifetime of a tool. This leads to a need to be able to make an easy transition to a replacement tool, something which integration should make less painful.

This paper looks in more detail at the issues involved and the integration technologies which can be used to resolve these issues.

2 INTEGRATION DEMANDS

The tools available to support software engineering have several things in common:

- they come from different vendors;
- they originate on different platforms and operating systems and are ported to other platforms and operating systems;
- they are based on different philosophies and employ different styles;
- they treat data as proprietary to the tool;
- they have their own priorities and timetables for enhancement of their functionality.

Against this backdrop we wish to be able to use a set of tools in a consistent and applicable fashion. To achieve this we must expect that we can get the tools to behave by:

- presenting a uniform user (presentation) interface;
- sharing data between tools;
- conforming to our view of the software engineering process;
- being controlled in a uniform manner;
- allowing portability across platforms.

All the above requirements would need to met by each tool for it to be true that any tool may be used in combination with any other set of tools. There are, however, two basic problems, the first being that each of the above points is not a simple Met/Not Met condition. Each point is quite complex and possibilities of meeting it cover the complete spectrum. The second problem is that different solutions are available to meet each of the above points and the chances of all the tools conforming to all the potential solutions is extremely unlikely.

Consequently it is necessary to think it terms of an integration framework which provides specific solutions to each of the integration issues. The tools are then expected to be integrated into the framework. The selection of the most appropriate framework for your needs will then be the determining factor in identification of the tools needed.

Choosing a framework is similar to the general issue of selecting hardware and software. The recommended approach is to choose your software and then select the hardware on the basis that it can run your software. However it is more common to see the selection of hardware occurring first, followed by the selection of software. The integration issue can be seen to have similar problems. The recommended approach would be to choose tools first and then to identify the appropriate integration framework in which to use them, however the more likely scenario is that of choosing the framework and then selecting tools from the set of tools which run within the framework.

3 INTEGRATION FRAMEWORK SERVICES

Providing an integration framework in which different tools can be incorporated requires a model like the one below which identifies the different services required to support integration. To be successful, it is reasonable that an integration framework must offer these integration services, which are explained in the following sections.

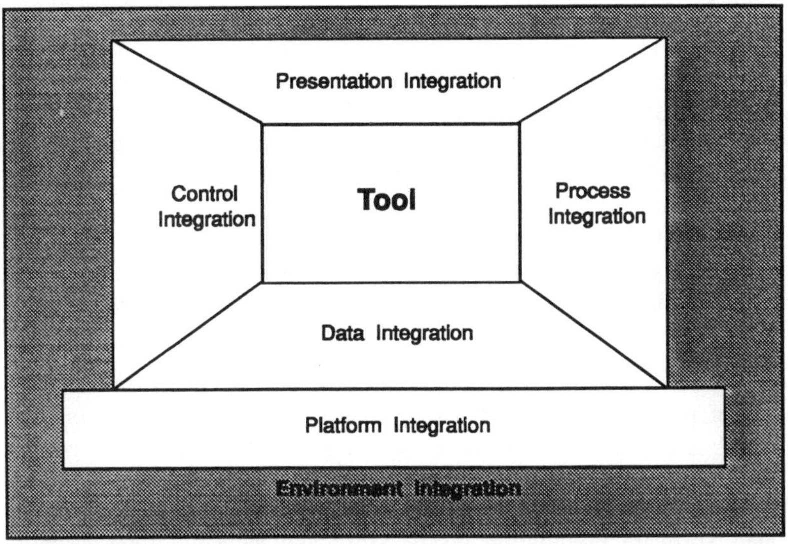

3.1 Presentation integration

Presentation or visual integration refers to the interface with the user of the tool. The interface may be for the purpose of invoking the tool or communicating with the tool as it performs its job.

For many years it has been common for hardware vendors to offer their own user interfacing tools and, in some cases, for software vendors to develop their own. On workstations, for example, it was possible to find different windowing systems on each platform, such as Display Manager on Apollo, UIS on DEC, X on HP, and Sunview on Sun. In the face of such diverse windowing systems different CASE vendors took different solutions. CADRE with Teamwork chose to develop their own windowing solution which was common across all the platforms on which Teamwork was found. This had the advantage of consistency when a user made use of Teamwork on multiple platforms, but meant the user needed to use two windowing systems, those of the platform and Teamwork. IDE chose to make their product, Software through Pictures, use the platform's native windowing system. For a user working on a single platform it meant that only one windowing system needed to be mastered, but a user on multiple platforms was less at home with the product. As the example illustrates, the problem of handling the different implementations of windowing systems was less than ideal, for both vendor and end-user.

In 1987 a significant number of companies agreed to standardise on an forthcoming release of MIT's X-Windows. Release 11 would offer a client/server based model for user interface management. Its appeal was caused by a number of factors including:

- the ability to run across a heterogeneous network, thereby allowing an application running on one platform to display its windows on another vendor's platform;
- it did not dictate the visual aspects of the user interface, frequently referred to as the desktop;
- the provision of a toolkit to build applications as well as the window management components;
- the definition of a standard interface between the different components of the standard, thereby permitting alternative implementations to be created which still complied with the X standard.

It took around two years for the consequences of this decision to manifest itself in terms of products supporting the X-Windows interface. These include both hardware-based products known as X-terminals and software-based products which employ X-Windows.

The Look and Feel element of the user interface has become dominated by the Open Software Foundation (OSF) Motif and the Unix International Open Look.

3.2 Data integration

Critical to tools working together is their ability to share data. Simple scenarios are that one tool generates output which is held as file which is then read by another tool. Alternatively the information may be piped between tools, but the implications are the same. The tool (or tools) which process the information must be informed of the structure and content of the interface. If the tool (or one of the tools) producing the output changes the structure or content of the interface, the tools which subsequently process it must also be changed to know about the changes to the interface.

This approach to data integration is far from perfect. It fails for the following reasons.

- The interface does not easily accommodate change without causing other tools involved to be impacted. This causes co-ordination issues when trying to manage Software Development Environments, which I think of as **Interface Ripple**. As one tool changes its output interface this causes other tools to change. Because they change it is likely they introduce changes to their output interfaces, thereby causing other tools to change. The co-ordination of this is particularly complicated when more than one tool can produce the output and/or more than one tool uses it as input.
- The interface is typically narrow. It is limited to the information thought by the producing tool to be needed. Over time the information needed will change. This causes change to the interface which leads to Interface Ripple.
- As the number of tools which participate in this point-to-point data integration increases, the problem of keeping the interface stable is exacerbated. Potentially there is a N(N-1)/2 number of integrations required – an impossible number.

The notion of an underlying database, typically referred to as a CASE Repository, is recognised as a superior solution. Tools would deposit information they create in the repository and extract from the repository required information which has been provided by other tools. Some of the issues relating to this approach include:

- Each tool may be providing information into the repository, but how is the repository structure defined? The concept of defining a meta-model (or metaschema) is normally proposed which leads to questions about who defines the meta-model, how is it extended, which tools provide which data to populate the meta-model etc.
- If we think of data residing in the repository as objects, we have the object's contents (which may be null) and information about the objects, which may be thought of as the object's attributes. The data which constitutes an object might be quite large (e.g. a program source) or quite small (e.g. a variable), with the object's attributes conveying information about the object to the outside world (of the object).

  The internals (or contents) of each object must be considered unstructured and thereby uninterpretable. The size (or granularity) of an object is important to the effectiveness of a repository. If objects are too coarse then it makes effective reuse more difficult as the information about the object is buried within its contents. Conversely, objects of too small a size may make the performance of the repository untenable.

- The definition of the repository in terms of objects must be considered a static definition, with information about how each tool manipulates the objects in the repository critical to understanding the dynamics of the repository.
  Each tool must offer some explanation of how it manipulates objects within the repository. This information may then be used to check the integrity of the repository and the viability of a specific set of tools working together in a specific configuration.
- Over time the versions of tools change and the definitions of objects also change. It is critical to the success of the repository that it is able to manage the evolution of both tools and objects as this is a characteristic of all but the simplest projects. On complex and lengthy projects it is frequently a requirement for different parts of the project to be able to operate with different versions of the same set of tools.

A more expansive view of these issues is presented in an article by Meyer.

3.3 Control integration

Combining tools together to make a viable software development environment requires mechanisms to control tools by offering facilities to register tools, invoke individual tools, perform tool composition and allow messages to be passed between tools or from tools to users. This last facility also requires mechanisms to support the registration of messages in terms of those generated by a specific tool and those consumed by a specific tool.

Tool registration is fundamental to having a CASE Framework which is independent of all functions except the intrinsic integration services. Each tool to be used, or new version of a tool, should be registered with the framework. Where a repository exists for data integration then the tool's view of the data should be an additional part of the registration process.

The ability to suspend or withdraw a tool should be available as well being able to place restrictions on the user communities which may invoke a tool. Initially it might be a requirement that a new tool be only available to a test group, with acceptance by the test group enabling the tool to be registered as generally available. Later on the tool may have its availability changed to existing projects only, so that all new projects are no longer able to invoke it.

Tool invocation should offer standardised mechanisms to invoke a specific tool as a new process. The ability to synchronise processes, suspend and resume processes should also be offered.

The ability to combine two or more tools into a higher-level process should be possible. This ability to perform tool composition may also be considered as part of process integration. For projects where the software developed is part of the manufacturing process and undergoes change in terms of functions or data, the ability to compose a higher-level software process based on the individual tools used in software development may be critical to automating the manufacturing process.

If true flexibility is expected in the CASE Framework it is important that different tools can take over different functions according to the user organisation's requirements. This requires some form of notification process such as tools being able to send and receive messages. The framework must offer mechanisms for tools to register the types of messages generated and the types of messages consumed. The registration process then allows the framework to route messages generated by one tool to the other tools which have indicated that they consume that type of message. This approach allows, for example, different project management tools to be registered within the framework without their introduction impacting on how other tools communicate with them.

Another mechanism for event notification are triggers within databases. Extending the repository to support triggers would mean that access to a particular object could cause some action, such as tool activation, to take place. The combination of triggers in the repository and message passing in the framework is not contradictory as the action of the trigger may be to invoke a message.

3.4 Process integration

Whilst data integration is the most complex integration issue, process integration is the least mature. Process integration itself could be kept separate from the framework to allow different tools to offer process integration as a service within the framework. This would almost certainly require the control integration services to offer a notification service such as messaging.

As we automate the process of software development we get further insights into what we do and how and why we do it, which is what Professor Zuboff identified as **informating.** Process Integration will offer facilities to model the process, manage the work-flows, identify the deliverables, and manage, in a sensitive manner, those involved in the development process. This will extend to users having **roles** which they take on when performing a particular function (e.g. developer, tester, manager), so that they are presented with a view of the system under development and the tools of the framework best suited to getting the job done. As development proceeds the views will change as necessary.

The services of process integration will allow the process that objects (in the repository) must follow to be modelled to ensure that they follow an optimal path for maximum productivity, quality and effectiveness.

For example, in a simplistic situation an object might present itself for review after being created. Users with the role reviewer may then be invited to participate in the review. On completion of the review the manager might receive details of the review whilst the object presents itself to a specific developer for rework. In the meantime notification of its process might be transmitted, via messages, to the project management tool so that the current schedule may be reviewed.

3.5 Platform integration

Many pressures exist for organisations to be capable of using a range of different computers and operating systems, considered here to be platforms. This pressure often requires the systems developed to be capable of running on different platforms and also for the tools used in development to be available on these different platforms.

Platform integration is the provision of a layer which sits between the individual tools and the operating system. It provides a consistent interface so that tools developed to that interface do not need to be modified when moved to a different platform which has the same platform integration layer.

There are software engineering initiatives such as PCTE working down to this problem, whilst broader initiatives such as ACE, OSF, POSIX, SVID2 are attacking this issue from the hardware architecture and operating system viewpoint.

3.6 Environment integration

The term Environment Integration is used here to describe the combination of all the other integration services. Integration into a framework product like those presented in this paper should be thought of as offering environment integration. The products offer some combination of presentation, data, control, process and platform integration and thereby reduce the need for individual tools to implement the different integration services directly.

The concept of a framework product may be thought of as offering the integration services outlined above. The provision of a tool into such a framework is determined by how it makes use of those services. In many situations it is necessary for the tool to be changed at the source code level for it to become framework compliant. To need internal changes to tools is a significant factor in delaying the adoption of frameworks.

A framework will only be universally accepted if it has a sufficient critical mass of tools which are compliant with it. In some quarters this issue has been recognised and encapsulation services offered. Encapsulation services provide a means by which a tool can be enclosed within a shell that interfaces the tool with the framework, enabling a non-compliant tool to appear compliant. Good encapsulation services can provide a fast-track route to an acceptable critical mass of tools for a framework and will be key to which frameworks succeed.

4 INTEGRATION TECHNOLOGIES AVAILABLE

This part of the paper takes a look at the initiatives taken and some standards which relate to integration, in addition to products which offer solutions to integration. These are listed in alphabetic order.

4.1 AD/Cycle

IBM has made a number of proposals to assist standardisation and integration. In one sense these culminate for commercial IS around AD/Cycle which is intended to provide support for the applications development cycle by allowing users to harness development tools from IBM and other vendors. With respect to the above mentioned integration services, it is only in the areas of presentation and data integration that AD/Cycle can be seen to help.

The tools work together through a central data repository where information created by tools is stored and retrieved by other tools as and when needed. To enable this concept to work requires the meta-model of the repository to be available so that tool developers are able to integrate their tools with the repository.

Presentation integration is represented by assuming the Common User Access (CUA) mantle inherited from the Systems Application Architecture (SAA). This assumes that tools will conform to a Presentation Manager style user interface.

Unfortunately there does not appear to be any support for encapsulation, either of a tool to give it a presentation manager-like user interface or to provide access to the repository.

4.2 AIX/CASE

IBM has for the RS6000 range not established a clear strategy to date. IBM has licensed SoftBench from Hewlett-Packard whilst also having a strong alliance with Atherton Technology, the suppliers of the Software BackPlane. Both SoftBench and the Software BackPlane are discussed separately. It could be that the choice of these two technologies is not just a case of covering two major options. Conjecture leads us to thinking that possibly IBM has some greater plan in the form of a SoftBench BackPlane, using what is best from the two products. This does have some merit but cannot be taken too seriously at present.

4.3 ATIS

A Tool Integration Service (ATIS) initially started as a joint proposal from Digital Equipment and Atherton Technology. It is viewed as a set of extensions to dictionary standards to improve support for CASE and is therefore primarily seen as aiding data integration.

ATIS identifies and defines a number of semantic models including a basic object-oriented data model, versioning model, configuration model and work-flow model. ATIS uses a layered model, like OSI, with the purpose of describing what is required, not how it is to be provided. The object-oriented data model allows object classes to be defined along with their methods. Objects may receive messages which invoke the appropriate method on the chosen object of that object class. Methods are the equivalent of functions which perform a known function (create, print, display...).

ATIS has been submitted to ANSI standards committee X3H4 as a proposed refinement of IRDS. It has also been proposed as the Object Management Layer for PCTE+.

An industry committee has been formed to promote ATIS. Known as CIS (CASE Information Services), it is responsible for refining ATIS and considering its relationship to various proprietary systems. CIS has around thirty members.

4.4 COHESION

COHESION is Digital's offering in the area of CASE Frameworks. It is primarily for VMS although it does include the FUSE offering for Ultrix (DEC's Unix). FUSE is discussed separately. Initially COHESION was simply a marketing banner for Digital's CASE products, and those of their third party vendors.

Recent developments have started to see COHESION change in the direction of a framework by offering the integration service facilities of CDD/Repository V5 and ACA Services.

CDD/Repository V5 has developed from their initial CDD product, the Common Data Dictionary, whose main purpose was to provide a language-independent means of defining data. In its latest incarnation it offers an ATIS interface in addition to its native CDD interface. It is based on an object-oriented model which enables it to be used to hold more complex objects than just data definitions. It is able to hold programs, databases, analysis and design models, etc. within the repository. CDD/Repository provides services to help support the system life cycle so, for example, it is possible to enforce project management policies.

The CDD/Repository Information Model is also being published, which will assist other tool vendors to integrate their products with the repository. The model is known as the Repository Information Model (RIM). The repository will allow new object definitions to be added to the repository, which will enable tool vendors to extend the basic information model. Although an important step forward it does imply a certain lack of control over the information model development which may well lead to incompatibilities in the repository when different tools are integrated.

Application Control Architecture (ACA) Services provide control level integration services. It offers the ability to invoke tools in a consistent way regardless of location (as long as it's on a Digital platform). It also provides a level of tool composition by allowing multiple tools to be invoked and used in a co-operative fashion.

It offers three levels of application interaction, the first two not requiring source code changes to the tool. The first level mechanisms are provided for registering and invoking independent tools across the network. Tools with existing command line or call interfaces can, at the second level of interaction, register a list of available functions across the network. This is achieved by encapsulated messages and methods which are separate to the tool. The available functions may then be used by other tools as and when requested. The final level of interaction requires source code changes. It provides a mechanism by which ongoing dialogues between tools may be conducted.

COHESION uses DECwindows/Motif but does not provide any means of encapsulating tools to allow them to conform to this interface.

4.5 EAST-*Environment*

From SFGL in France, it is described as a management-oriented IPSE (Integrated Project Support Environment). It offers many of the integration services that can be expected from a CASE Framework. EAST-*Environment* was developed as part of the Eureka project through the co-operative development effort of SFGL, Nokia, DMR, Datamat, Intecs, Systemi and Bull-HN.

It is based upon the PCTE (Portable Common Tools Environment) which is discussed later. Due to its PCTE underpinning it is able to offer data level, control level and platform level integration. PCTE uses X-Windows as its windowing system and East offers the OSF/Motif user interface toolkit to develop X-based tools.

Integration of tools is possible through encapsulation. Encapsulation in East provides for tool activation, interfacing to the PCTE Object Management System and with the OSF/Motif user interface without the need to make source code changes.

Process integration services are offered via the Process Management Services. These allow process models to be defined, tasks to be allocated to team members, and for the workload of each task to be monitored and controlled. A number of Off-the-shelf Process Models may also be used as is, or undergo further refinement.

4.6 Entreprise II

Entreprise II is also from France, in this case SYSECA. It describes itself as the open IPSE. Like EAST it is also based on PCTE. Entreprise II originates from a project with the French Ministry of Defence, ITI Group and Thompson-CSF.

Given its PCTE foundation it is able to offer data level, control level and platform level integration. PCTE uses X-Windows as its windowing system and Entreprise II offers presentation level integration through OSF/Motif or Open Look user interface toolkits.

A toolkit for encapsulating and integrating tools is provided. Known as the Entreprise II backplane it offers services for window and dialogue management, data dictionary access, all PCTE facilities, and an integrated command language.

4.7 FUSE

From Digital, it is positioned as part of COHESION but in reality must be considered separately. It is sometimes viewed as a tool set for Ultrix users in which case it is not a framework. However it offers some integration services which lead it towards being a CASE Framework. At present these integration services are different to those offered in the rest of COHESION so it is necessary to consider them separately.

At the presentation integration level FUSE offers the OSF/Motif user interface toolkit. At present no encapsulation facilities are offered to support presentation integration although a recent announcement has stated that encapsulation facilities will be offered.

The only other integration service offered is a notification mechanism for control level integration. This uses the Multicast Message Server (MCMS) to provide a message broadcasting service. This would appear to conflict with the services offered by ACA Services.

4.8 PCTE

PCTE is both a standard and an implementation. PCTE originates from the European ESPRIT programme which started in 1984. Release 1.4 was made in 1986, followed in 1988 with release 1.5. To date most implementations of PCTE have been by, or in collaboration with, GIE Emeraude.

Its route to becoming a standard has been rather torturous. The initial versions of PCTE were seen by many as too Unix-like. In 1987 a project called PCTE+ was initiated. Its goal was to define the adaptations required to make it suitable for developing high-security systems. In the same timeframe ECMA were considering the standardisation of PCTE. The results of PCTE+ definition phase provided a revised specification with Ada interface definitions in addition to those for C. In December 1990 the standard ECMA Specification 149 was released based upon the results of PCTE+. This is seen as a stepping-stone towards obtaining an ISO standard.

As an implementation PCTE must be viewed as a building block for CASE Frameworks, rather than a framework in its own right. This view is confirmed by PCTE being the basis of both EAST and Enterprise II, whilst SoftBench from Hewlett-Packard is undergoing further development to make it PCTE compliant.

PCTE is currently positioned as being the Open Repository, although this seems to devalue many other aspects. The repository of PCTE is an Object Management System (OMS) based on the Entity-Relationship-Attribute model. The meta-model for the repository allows for extension and is defined through Schema Definition Sets (SDS) which are held as part of the OMS. No global schema exists to represent the meta-model, instead the meta-model is part of the OMS as represented by the union of SDSs.

Control integration is supported through mechanisms to start a tool, manage processes and perform basic event notification.

Platform integration is offered through the provision of language bindings in C and Ada, with support for distribution and environment management. It is these features which offer much of the portability symbolised by the name PCTE.

Presentation integration is offered by an Application-Programmer interface (API) based on the X-Windows system. The choice of OSF/Motif or Open Look as the window manager is not made by PCTE, the requirement being that the window manager be compliant with the X-lib interface.

4.9 SoftBench

SoftBench is from Hewlett-Packard and represents a watershed in the approach to software development by the major hardware vendors. The watershed has nothing to do with technology, instead it is the change in philosophy it represents. HP have made SoftBench available on Sun Sparcstations and also licensed the SoftBench technology to IBM for use on the RS6000 workstation platform. Other products from the hardware vendors have appeared on other platforms but the significance is that this is a product extremely close to the core of software development and represents a significant change of attitude.

SoftBench offers presentation integration based on OSF/Motif with provision of encapsulation technology, which allows tools to be made OSF/Motif compliant often without the need for source code changes.

Control integration is offered through the Broadcast Message Service (BMS). Like the Multicast Message Server of FUSE, the technology for BMS originates at Brown University from the Field Environment project.

Whilst no platform level integration services currently exist, it could be argued that such integration is available indirectly due to its availability on several platforms.

4.10 Software BackPlane

The Software BackPlane from Atherton Technology has been an important forerunner in establishing solutions to many aspects of integration and pushing the market forward. The product is available on many platforms and Atherton has strong relationships with both DEC and IBM.

With Digital they developed the initial ATIS proposal and continue to push things forward via the CIS Consortium.

Presentation integration level is based on OSF/Motif although no provision is made for encapsulating tools.

Data integration is achieved via the Software BackPlane Repository, a model with, as one would expect, a lot in common with the ATIS object-oriented model.

Control integration is available for standardised tool invocation and basic event notification.

Process level integration is offered through the ability to define work-flows.

Like SoftBench, platform integration is indirectly supported by its availability on many platforms.

The Software BackPlane provides encapsulation technology to allow data to be registered with the repository but not held in the repository, and also for the repository to register and contain the data.

4.11 Product comparison

To provide an At a Glance view, the following table compares the framework products described above.

	Integration Services				
Product	**Presentation**	**Control**	**Process**	**Data**	**Platform**
AD/Cycle	✘	✘	✘	✔	✘
AIX/SoftBench	✔	✔	✘	✘	✘
AIX/S-BackPlane	✘	✔	✔	✔	✘
COHESION	✘	✔	✔	✔	✘
EAST	✔	(PCTE)	✔	(PCTE)	(PCTE)
Enterprise II	✔	(PCTE)	✔	(PCTE)	(PCTE)
FUSE	(✔)	✔	✘	✘	✘
PCTE	✘	✔	✘	✔	✔
SoftBench	✔	✔	✘	✘	✘
Software BackPlane	✘	✔	✔	✔	✘

Note: The Presentation column is based on whether the framework product offers an encapsulation facility to enable foreign tools to comply with the framework's presentation interface.

5 CONCLUSION

Significant progress has been made in recent years on the issue of how to provide a framework in which a diverse range of tools from a diverse range of suppliers can be incorporated in such a way as to make them feel as if they were designed and implemented by a single supplier.

The products on the market generally do not support all the necessary aspects of integration to offer a complete solution, although through the merger or co-operation of these solutions it is possible to see fully functional frameworks becoming available by the mid '90s if not earlier.

Throughout the paper much has been mentioned about encapsulation technology. It is, I feel, the key to achieving a significant breakthrough. It is evident that there will be a number of competing framework products which will be attempting to get tool suppliers to provide their tools in their frameworks. This will continue to put pressure on tool suppliers as to which frameworks to support – which will no doubt lead to politically-based, as against technology-based, decisions determining the winners and losers. Encapsulation technology could be the key by enabling tool suppliers, or end-user organizations, to integrate a tool into a framework without the need for changes to the source code of the tool.

It is unlikely, however, that encapsulation technology can fully succeed in this area, particularly in the area of platform integration, without tool suppliers taking more care and paying more attention to the internal tool architecture as identified by Tony Wasserman. Without the correct internal architecture it is difficult for tools to be adapted to fit in with differing framework products, and in some cases will make it impossible to perform integration without source code changes.

Another area where advances need to be made is message registration in event notification schemes which employ broadcast messaging mechanisms (e.g. BMS). The specification of message definitions to avoid overlap and underlap must be managed along with support for checking the integrity of a specific environment. For example, a message is expected but never arrives!

It is also important that repositories be extendable to accommodate change. Similar issues of integrity arise. If data is deposited is it used? Or worse: if data is expected has it been deposited?

One further concern to express is that of framework suppliers offering tools to allow partially populated frameworks to exist. This is an interesting problem as without some tools a framework is of no use. To this end most framework suppliers have developed tools to work within the framework, thereby increasing its initial value whilst gaining insight into the problems of integration. The potential consequence is that other tool suppliers with tools that compete against the framework supplier's tools may be discouraged from investing to make their tools compliant with the framework. Something of a Catch 22, it may nonetheless lead to a restricted choice of tools for the framework – the opposite of what is desired.

The increasing availability and use of frameworks will see further issues arise, however these experiences will be as the result of some positive steps forward.

REFERENCES

ANSI X3.138 (1988) Information Resource Dictionary System, ANSI.

Daley, R. (1991) Tool Integration Survey Results, *ToolInfo*, the bulletin of the StP UK User Group (4) pp. 23–32.

Humphrey, W. (1989) *Managing the Software Process,* Addison Wesley.

Meyer, S. (1991) Difficulties in Integrating Multiview Development Systems, *IEEE Software*, 8 (1), pp. 49–57.

Reiss, S. (1990) Connecting Tools Using Message Passing in the Field Environment, *IEEE Software*, 7 (4) pp. 57–66.

Thomas, I. (1989) PCTE Interfaces: Supporting Tools in Software Engineering Environments, *IEEE Software*, 6 (6), pp. 15–23.

Wasserman, A. (1990) Software Engineering Environments, *Tool Integration in Software Engineering Environments*, pp 137–149, Verlag.

Zuboff, S. (1989) *In the Age of the Smart Machine: The Future of Work and Power*, Butterworths.

2 Integration. Why Bother?

Alan J. Gater
Oracle Corporation

Over the past half century Computers and Computer technology have pervaded every aspect of industrialised society. The rate of progress has been phenomenal, even in a century where phenomenal technical progress has been the norm – and, in fact, most of the recent advances in manufacturing, transport and communications etc. have only been possible because of the advances in computing. An inevitable result of this explosion of creativity and ingenuity has been the appearance of many discrete and disparate pockets of application. The plethora of CASE tools now coming to the forefront of our attention seem to have inherited all the rebellious aspects of their parent industry. Is it now time to mould these brilliant and wayward children into model citizens, or should evolution be allowed to follow its natural course, with only the fit surviving?

1 SO WHAT'S THE PROBLEM?

Some years ago I gave up a secure job in a software house and went into business with a friend developing software tools for PRESTELviewdata users (yes, that many years ago).

I bought an Apple II microcomputer and learned Basic and Motorola 6200 assembler; then a modem and a telephone and then... problems. How was I going to get the information being squirted down the line by the Post Office into my little Apple. So I asked another friend of mine (the sort you always find round the back of things with a soldering iron) what he thought. 'No problem, what you need's an aisher.' (Which I later found to be an ACIA – Asynchronous Communications Interface Assembly).

John (my friend) built me a thing full of pins and wire wraps and plugged it into the Mother Board, and told me that if I 'polled the strobe' at this port address I could pick incoming characters up, and that if I poked characters I wanted to send out into another port address these would get sent. This was all magic to me, having spent the previous six years writing stacks of COBOL and avoiding like the plague anything to do with Hardware.

Oddly enough, it worked.

That was when I hit the real problem. The messages coming down the line just came. Viewdata text is funny stuff, full of control characters for colour switches and font switches and changes of mode from character to graphical – with a <CR> cancelling all previous instructions. And the only map I had was the picture on the Viewdata terminal of what the message should look like and a long string of the characters that made that message in my own file on the Apple.

An interesting puzzle, but one that, in the event, only took a few days to sort out.

I was very proud, and realised then that with a bit of imagination, electric string, and a will to succeed I could make anything talk to anything.

Some few years after this I became Systems and Programming Manager for an insurance company and had the responsibility for selecting and evaluating software and hardware solutions for future business systems developments. What a maze. It was quite easy to find off-the-shelf solutions for many of our requirements when each was taken in isolation. But integrate them? Some of the hair-brained schemes presented by eager salespeople for filling in the holes in their particular offerings make me laugh. Now.

It wasn't just the volume and complexity of the integration work that stopped me, though that was bad enough, but the various vendors – either from protectionism or plain good sense – were not in the least bit happy about me gluing their products together in my own sweet fashion. In the end we settled for far less than our development strategy called for – and our strategy was not particularly ambitious.

I came to understand that I had been congratulating myself for solving the wrong problem when I had bread-boarded my PRESTEL interface. Sure I could make anything talk to anything, but the **real** requirement was to make sure **everything** could talk to **everything**.

Since then I have tried to champion appropriate standardisation and the integration of technologies and disciplines across the industry wherever possible. Of course 'appropriate' is very subjective.

2 WHAT DO WE MEAN BY INTEGRATION?

I followed the standard form in these matters and looked up the word in the dictionary (the Penguin English as it was nearest to hand) and extracted the following definition: Integrate: To form or blend into a whole.

I feel quite happy with this as a starting point. The words 'form' and 'blend' have comfortable undertones of seamlessness and 'a whole' implies completeness.

So what is this whole that we are striving for?

As we are talking here about the development of effective computer systems, I could state my 'whole' as being the capability of taking a **systems** requirement, defined in terms that the person having the requirement understands, through to a **systems** solution which that same person can use.

The next step is to identify what the components of such a whole are – and here things get more difficult.

Computers have proved so adaptable that they have permeated every aspect of industrialised life. The uses to which this technology is put increases faster than my ability to catalogue them. The key factor here, I believe, is to identify a 'whole' that is more valuable than the sum of its parts.

Let me paint a picture.

Fred, working at his desk, queries a Form style screen of all the quarterly results to date for salespeople in his region. He prints out a formatted hard copy of the results to take to his meeting, and also directs an e-mail copy of the results to George, his Sales Director.

George reads this mail, and the reports from his other sales managers, and loads all the data directly into his spreadsheet. He applies his own forecasting algorithm to the current quarter's data, based on data about the spread of sales in each of the previous four quarters, extracted directly from the corporate data pool and automatically correlated against the base data loaded from the mails. Things look a bit bad so he charts the result as a histogram and mails it to Charles, the MD.

Charles is out of town at the moment, negotiating a hugely expensive deal, but he has left a forwarding address of 'The Fax Machine, Luxurious Hotel, Palm Springs' to which this communication is automatically forwarded. Fortunately Charles reads his Fax in the nick of time and takes the next plane home (economy, of course).

This degree of integration is well within our current capability. We have already built each component. We already know exactly how to tie the pieces together. The network is already in place. Our users see such systems demonstrated every week on Horizon or Tomorrow's World. But no user has access to a system that actually allows him to do these things without direct manual intervention at nearly every step. And they are dissatisfied.

So where does the problem lie?

3 HOW DID IT GET THIS WAY?

In the early days the computer was a calculator capable of carrying out multi-step computations. Nothing more and nothing less. The user was a mathematician and the requirement was the resolution of some calculation performed on a number of variables. As a 'whole' solution it was a failure. The 'programme' had to be hard-wired and rewired for every task. This forced the users to define their requirements in terms that the programmer understood and to go back to that programmer every time they wanted any slight correction or change.

The next generation of computers introduced the major new concept that laid the ground for the more versatile machines we are now familiar with; programs in 'software'. This development allowed the mathematicians, used to formal ways of defining their problems, direct access to the means of resolving those problems – though still not in their own 'natural language'.

However, at the same time, these more versatile machines also became capable of more general data processing, opening the door to a different type of user with less easily defined requirements and with less aptitude for formal definition of process. Instead of getting rid of the Programmer we had introduced the Analyst – and the process of disintegration had been established.

Each advance in computer technology, whilst increasing the power and capability of the machines, also increased the specialisation of the new technical elite. Operating systems gave us the Operator. More sophisticated operating systems gave us the Systems Programmer, whilst mass storage and hard-copy devices kept the Operator anyway. File management systems needed designers, TP systems introduced screen ergonomists and UI specialists etc. All these experts widened the gap between the users with their requirements and the means of their satisfaction, each link in the chain another potential weak spot.

Business systems have become critical to enterprises and, therefore, the timeliness and predictability of the delivery of solutions is also critical – and with so many cooks seasoning this particular broth it takes a master chef to ensure a palatable dish; enter the Project Manager.

The technology itself has advanced in disjointed leaps and bounds, introducing a whole raft of technical specialists, originally completely divorced from the traditional development of users solutions and devoted wholly to servicing the technology itself: Comms Engineers, Database Administrators, Operations Analysts, Information Centre Specialists, Support Consultants, the list is endless. In the mean time, the user profile changed as did their requirements, bringing these disciplines firmly back into the mainstream of business systems development.

So we have a situation where there are now several thousands of bits of technology that we could, sensibly, propose as objects for integration, coupled with dozens (at least) of disciplines and specialist skills required to apply these technologies.

4 WHOSE FAULT IS IT?

Some of this disintegration is simply inexcusable and has resulted from protectionism and conservatism. We have also been guilty of extreme narcissism. The industry is fascinated by its own technology and has been selling, in the main, to DIY enthusiasts who are equally fascinated by the technology. (I was recently involved in a sales situation where the main criteria for selection of a data-management system were, firstly, the best 2-phase commit strategy and, secondly, the most glamorous object-oriented futures. Never once was a business requirement voiced that needed a distributed solution, nor any particular use defined for Objects – and all the members of the evaluation committee were IT specialists.)

On the other hand, a lot of the disintegration was simply inevitable, resulting from the incredible rate of growth of an immature industry. Just too much going on. Whatever the cause, the result has been that the adaptability of the technology, coupled with massive increase in power and dramatic reduction in cost, has created an environment where capability has far exceeded our users' current ability to assimilate and utilise it and the Industry's ability to profitably market it.

Because of the incredible rate of progress some concepts and, therefore, the technology that supports those concepts, simply becomes outdated. Eight bit architectures and 256 codes were great before it became economically feasible to store and process gigabytes of data, but increase the volume of data and add the Kanji character set into the equation and this just doesn't cut the mustard any more.

On the technology side, finding an integrated solution is mostly a matter of waiting. The more separate components one needs in one's integrated solution the longer the wait is likely to be – but if the capability is not yet available to you, then it isn't available to your competitors either. And if the need (or the reward) is great you can always fund the development yourself.

It is tempting to blame the technologists for our problems, but I think that would be unfair. My example in the previous section is quite supportable with current technology. Almost as soon as two technologists create things that can be integrated, an entrepreneurial third finds some way of gluing them together in an inventive and potentially useful way.

5 WHY, IF THE CAPABILITY IS AVAILABLE, CAN'T WE USE IT?

Put simply, demand (and ambition) has outstripped supply. The Industry was complacent and comfortable in its control of the market, then the market changed.

This is not a new problem. History abounds with myths or facts about different industries' attempts to control, or at least keep in balance, supply and demand. I was raised on stories of Xerox buying and suppressing new copying process patents, and certainly cars could be more efficient and environmentally friendly. Inevitably the result has been that, at some point, Pandora's Box is opened and the new thing is marketed by someone, or the consumers become aware that they are being short changed, and the Industry gets turned on its head for a while.

The herald of this new dissatisfaction with the computer industry in the business community was the PC. While the dinosaurs of business computing were dolling out crumbs, the poor users have been desperately trying to get the business done and discovered desktop computing. On the surface this looked like the answer to many of the disintegration problems: just the user, his requirement and the means to its solution. But in many ways the end-user computing revolution has merely highlighted the problems. Single user desktop computing ran out of steam before it really got started. Users found they wanted to share word-processing templates with other users, and couldn't. They wanted to get access to corporate data, and couldn't. They wanted to use inter-office electronic mail, and couldn't. They had got hold of a handsaw, but still couldn't make planks out of trees.

But on the plus side this revolution cut out all (well, most) of the middle men for a while and made our users more computer literate. This has forced a complete re-evaluation of usability and has spawned a whole raft of useful business packages that 'do the job'. It has empowered our users to voice articulately their manifest dissatisfaction where previously they could only seethe. And it gave them the most powerful argument of all – they could withdraw their custom.

The first response to this new, louder, consumer voice was a relatively massive upswing in 'Open' systems. Operating systems like Unix and languages like C (which are fundamentally unsuitable for most business developments) gained popularity simply because they **did** allow consumers greater choice of supplier and they did interconnect (well, better than that which had gone before). The second response was the sudden increase in the market for connectivity tools. The first-time-buyer market was quickly used up and, anyway, they mostly didn't have the huge IT budgets of the established companies. Most of the best prospects for these new, desirable, cheap boxes already had a massive investment in mainframes that they couldn't just abandon. Now, of course, we are seeing the effort being put into the provision of Mac style 'desktop' interfaces and WYSIWYG tools that allow the PC-educated user to operate in this new and larger environment.

Just having the technology, though, doesn't mean we know how to use it. We have been building 'integrated' business solutions for many years. The vast majority of the systems developed for business were, in fact, adequate. They supported the businesses, reduced costs, and allowed entry into new fields that could not have been tackled without the use of such technology. However we, the computer industry, have been incredibly successful in fanning the fears of our consumers; that if they don't use our latest technology now their competitors will, to their own advantage. It is true that there are now enough cases of winners who did and losers who didn't to show that these fears are justified. Less well publicised are the, possibly equally frequent, cases of users who **did** employ the latest technology too soon, and lost because of it.

Still, the technology is there. And the user demand is that we, the suppliers, should now be able to apply it to their needs quickly. This no longer looks like a problem. It looks like a golden opportunity, the prize going to those who can find the means of letting the user community adopt this technology soonest in the most effective ways.

6 WHAT CAN WE DO ABOUT IT?

The theme here is CASE Integration. I haven't spoken much about CASE yet. CASE is Computer Aided Systems (or Software, depending on your viewpoint) Engineering. The key words here are Computer Aided. It has taken a long time for us to realise that the technology we have been selling to industry to solve its cost and efficiency problems applies just as well to our own industry. The classic cobbler's child syndrome.

I mentioned the spawning of the multiple development disciplines and skills that accompanied the advances in technology. This disintegration of process was unavoidable, desirable even. The specialisation of the development roles and processes into the number of disciplines and life-cycle phases most of us are familiar with is just the best way people have found of breaking a big, complex, task down into smaller, manageable chunks. There has been a price paid (by the user of course) in that every transition between disciplines and phases has allowed dilution of understanding and the introduction of errors.

The techniques we have historically used have been begged, borrowed and stolen from the construction and manufacturing industries and have been adapted as necessary to the, essentially R&D, practice of systems development. As the industry has matured, and the ways in which computer systems can be applied in industry has expanded, techniques and disciplines have evolved which are wholly the province of IT, formal data analysis *à la Chen* probably being at the forefront of these. Names like Demarco, Youdan, Jackson, Martin etc. are known to all in the industry as originators of new and better ways of tackling the development process, either through revolutionary insights or evolutionary ways of applying them.

There is no doubt that the adoption, over the last decade, of formal and structured development methods by the majority of the industry has allowed us to tackle bigger and bigger projects with greater relative degrees of success. Our problem now is that our rate of advance, when compared with that of the technology, is too slow.

There is now a vast choice in development methods and techniques – methods being mostly the sequence and control of the development process and techniques being the most appropriate way to carry out a particular activity within that process.

Right now the methods employed almost universally are simply variations on the 'Development Life Cycle' theme I was introduced to twenty years ago, i.e. establish what the requirement is, analyse the detail of the required process, design a mechanism to support that process, write code to apply that process, test it, run it and regret it.

The techniques, however, have become vastly more sophisticated. The ways in which we model data, events and functions (the staples of systems) have moved very much away from the black art side of things almost to a science – my definition of a science being that which allows the practitioner to predict a result prior to its being proven by experiment, rather than just diving in and getting your hands grubby. Our difficulty is not so much that we don't know what to do than that, like the mathematician of the '40s, our problems are just getting to big too solve by hand.

As with so many good ideas, it is very difficult to pinpoint a source. Certainly James Martin seems to be generally credited as the father of CASE and without doubt he has done most to promote his concept. The reality, though, is undoubtedly that the idea had just found its time. In the US CASE vendors (where the CASE acronym was coined) were applying CAD-CAM (Computer Aided Design and Manufacturing) technology to the various diagramming analysis and design techniques. In Europe the emphasis was on developing the Operating System model to encompass more development tools (including, unfortunately, the traditional less-than-friendly operating-system user interface) to produce IPSE. ICL, probably alone at the time, applied the new Network Database technology to produce a Developers Database or Dictionary. Others, compiler and language vendors, were spearheading the development of more declarative languages to speed up the coding process. And I shouldn't understate the enormous and valuable input to all of this from the academic institutions.

The pattern has been very much in a parallel to that of the development of the technology itself, as has the result. It is as difficult to define what CASE is now as it is to define a computer. Certainly our current concept of the 'Computer' is far more encompassing than just a multi-step arithmetic processor. If we just look at the humble PC, each box includes I/O devices – the keyboard and screen; some mass storage device – the fixed disk; in all likelihood it will contain a maths co-processor – another entirely separate computer to our old way of thinking. It may have its operating system in firmware or software and it may contain sophisticated character generators. Recently SUN Microsystems coined the phrase 'The Network IS The Computer'.

The modern computer is a miracle of integration. Yet it is clear, when one looks at the uses computers are put to, that not only **can** there not be a single hardware/software solution but also that their **shouldn't** be. Ignoring the commodity uses of computing like digital watches and pocket calculators, the best configuration for an insurance company is never going to be the same as that required by the meteorological office. They may both need to capture data directly from geographically distant locations, store the data locally and apply some algorithm to that data for display of results on an output device. The computers they use may be based on the same chips. The software may even be written in the same language, but the devices they each need to attach, the data they need to process, and the processes they apply to that data are fundamentally different. Each can be satisfied by more or less the same technology, but the 'whole' that they need is based on a different integration model. So the argument for integration is really one for cross-product connectivity between different suppliers' offerings.

The same thing is true of CASE. The original CAD-based CASE tools have provided a generic heading for the family of computer-based tools that support the development of systems. CASE now seems to encompass CAD-type applications, data dictionary and, to an extent, code generators. However, IBM have added repository services to the list (a very IPSE like concept), SABRE have added compilers and interactive debuggers, Atherton Technologies' BackPlane product introduced the common interface concept, now very much the goal of the PCTE initiative, and my own company (Oracle) is firmly placing project management and strategic business analysis tools (as would be used by management accountants to determine **what** to develop) on the list.

In many ways the CASE heading stands not so much for an identifiable product as for the integration of all these computer-based development aids into a single, coherent whole. And, as with the 'Computer Integration' argument, the requirement is not so much for CASE integration as for cross-product connectivity between different vendors' tools.

6.1 Why is interconnectivity necessary?

A good method will provide a consistent framework for Systems development, allowing for the use of different techniques at each stage depending on the desired result, and a good technique can be adapted to many different circumstances. But no one method or set of techniques is right for everything. And no one method or set of techniques is right for all time.

That explosion of technology which resulted in all these development 'trades' is also providing mechanisms to make many of them redundant. The original Chen Entity Modelling technique has been refined to the point where many of the process rules and constraints can be extrapolated directly from the analysis model, and database technology – relational and object oriented – is reaching the point where those abstract concepts can be directly implemented without requiring the traditional skills of the DB designer or the programmer.

Of course this doesn't help the real-time system designer much. And, of course, the data modeller now has to be very highly skilled indeed.

On the other side of the equation, the requirements of users have now introduced the dimensions of real location and local time – aspects of systems ignored in our current techniques for dealing with data, events and functions.

The application of computer technology to the process of development is having much the same affect as OLTP had on the punch operator. We removed the requirement for one skill but replaced it with several others. As our CASE tools become more powerful and more integrated, the gap between definition of requirement and realisation of solution is decreasing. However, the number of possible requirements and the choice of appropriate solutions multiplies daily. And the advances don't happen all at once. Just because there is an advance in one field doesn't mean we should have to trade in our whole development environment and start again. Nor does it mean that every vendor's tool is no longer viable. It just suggests that there may be another component to integrate into our revised model of a desirable whole. And with advances coming mainly from the vendor community, no single vendor can possibly be current in all areas at one time.

Training developers is too expensive to allow us to switch radically from one approach to another. I am not one who believes that a box with square corners and a line with an arrow head is intrinsically more meaningful than a box with rounded corners and a line with a crow's foot. But if I have just spent time and effort on teaching my staff to speak the language of squares and arrows I am very unwilling to pull the rug out from under them, especially as there is no intrinsic value in the symbols used. But I will be very unhappy if this justifiable protection of my investment results in my not having access to the new tools that will keep me competitive in my market.

7 WHOSE JOB IS IT?

Now that we have established that what we mean by Integration is interconnectivity it becomes easier to identify mechanisms for achieving it.

It is not only unreasonable to expect all vendors to adhere to a single model of what CASE is, it would be unwise. CASE, like the technology it uses and helps exploit, is not a static thing. To force, even for a short while, a single definition onto the vendors and users would be a great disservice and would stifle the very advances that are needed.

In the technology arena interconnectivity was achieved by vendors publishing the interfaces to their devices and encouraging others to exploit them. Out of this have emerged, initially, niche markets for interconectivity tools and, eventually, *de facto* standards. As the standard runs out of steam, as invariably it does, the industry enters another round of non-standard but enhanced interfaces, the niche markets grow, and eventually a new standard emerges.

This pattern is healthy and, probably, the only way to allow things to advance.

This is not to say that the standards bodies do not have a role to play because they obviously do. Their task is to encourage and lengthen the periods of stability, and to shorten the periods of instability. They achieve this by providing a forum for evaluation of both users' stated requirements and current vendors' offerings. By publishing standards they help to protect the customer at two levels.

Firstly, they provide the customer with a vocabulary and a yardstick for product evaluation. Without even approaching a vendor the customer can begin to put together a coherent shopping list. S/he can then ask the vendor, 'Does your product conform to standard xyz?' If it does then they should now be aware of what they are buying. If it does not then the onus is on the vendor to define in what ways the product fails to met the standard. Either way the customer is better placed to determine whether or not this product will meet their requirement.

Secondly, by encouraging the customer to ask for a product that meets the defined standard they have helped to promote both the standard and its longevity – the vendor has to be pretty certain that their offering is better than the standard before going their own sweet way. This helps to protect the customer's investment.

This system is far from perfect and, as with all good ideas, it has its failings. One dominant supplier can lock the customer in to its own, unratified, *de facto* standard and flaunt the preferred one.This looks OK until you hit the first brick wall and find you are in too deep to get out, or the standards body can just miss the mark completely, as happened with the ANSI IRDS Standard V1. Instead of defining a baseline of service and a common interface they defined a product that nobody wanted to build or buy.

While the standards bodies serve an invaluable purpose, their remit is not to define the standard up front but to ratify it once it is proved to be of worth. Without the active participation of the vendors **and** the user community they can serve neither party well.

The key to integration is not one model, or even one supplier, it is Open Interfaces. If a vendor is not prepared to publish the interface to its tool then don't buy it. If a vendor **has** published the interface to its tool, then it just takes a bit of imagination, electric string, and a will to succeed and anything can be made to talk to anything.

8 WHY BOTHER?

IT is now the single largest industry in the world, having, in the last year, finally overtaken the automotive industry. There is very little that we can currently imagine that we cannot already demonstrate the technical capability of achieving. Yet the most common complaint of users, the people spending these hundreds of billions of dollars, is that they cannot buy that which they can see could be readily available and which they believe they desperately need.

The industry has bucked trends and got away with its self-fascination and indifference to consumer demands for far longer than reason should dictate – in the main, I believe, because of the dominance over the last four decades of one major player, dominance to the point where it has been in a position to dictate to the market what it can have and should want. Those days are definitely over. The way is open for the user community not to change masters but to become the masters.

The market is not only too big now for one supplier to go it alone, in the current climate the consumer community will no longer allow it: they have to protect their now not inconsiderable investment in CASE. And in an industry where change is the norm, co-existence with the new is the only mechanism the vendors have for protecting their own, now not inconsiderable, development investment in CASE.

Why integrate? Whether you are a user or a supplier, if you don't integrate someone else will. Rugged individualism is the route to extinction.

3 The Future Direction for Integration Technology

Cheryll S. Gerelle
IBEX Computing SA, Archamps, France

1 INTRODUCTION

Relatively few organizations are making use of CASE frameworks. The current users tend to be from an elite group of people working on large projects and are, to some extent, the most Software Engineering and CASE literate. As tools which support the development process and software engineering practices become more widely used, I predict an upsurge in the use of integration technology.

How will the integration technology of today evolve if frameworks are to be used by the masses? For one thing, integration technology will need to become much more accessible to the layman. This will mean simplifying the process of tools integration, educating users and helping them become more productive by producing higher quality systems than they do today.

For tools and framework providers, quasi-standards may need to emerge before full-fledged ones are available and a wide choice of compliant tools on the market. This means that current framework providers have the challenge of getting this technology accepted into the market. Systems integrators have a key role to play with the technology providers in surmounting these challenges.

2 SIMPLIFYING THE PROCESS OF TOOLS INTEGRATION

There are many integration models being talked about today, from various reference models to vendor specific models. There are two major similarities between most of these models: they all have the same basic functionality and they are all difficult to use, except for trained computer specialists.

While the thought of what a framework provides (standard interfaces to tools, information sharing between tools, built in controls over the environment, just to name a few) is commendable, there is no easy way to give the user freedom to select tools or update tools with newer versions without relying on professional computing staff. One of the big challenges for framework vendors will be to make these tasks easier.

Simple user interfaces, like the one on the Macintosh™, have brought computing to a wider audience. Complicated commands are masked by icons and draw and drop facilities. If integration frameworks are to have the same profound effect, then they too must use similar techniques. Imagine having all of your tools displayed as icons and literally dropping them into the framework of your choice by a click of the mouse on your workstation.

Of course now, with integrated voice we might visualize the progression even further. Why drag the icons into the framework, simply tell the the ones you are interested in to go into the framework.

A further development of integration technology might be the use of expert systems to create intelligent frameworks. These frameworks would configure the best environment for the type of application being developed. The user would only verbally describe his needs.

Application builders and simulation tools would be a prime part of the tool set for intelligent frameworks so that different scenarios could be played out quickly, results analyzed and the best choices made.

3 EDUCATION

Education facilities within the frameworks and tools could be expected to grow and utilize newer techniques such as multi-media. Two groups need training, the users and the computer professionals who will need to maintain the products.

I predict that live video with built-in query facilities, either through clicking on a mouse or by voice, will replace much of the conventional user documentation. By opening a video window on the workstation, a user will be given an interactive tutorial on the tools or the frameworks. They will be able to interactively create applications as part of the tutorial and see these working in a separate window.

The help facilities will allow them to seek additional information from a built-in encyclopedia. Simulated drawings will show how information is being shared between tools when user-activated commands are given.

The definition of workstation will extend to being both the work and education environment for people on the job. This easy access to educational materials will put another challenge on suppliers to promote their products through video disks as opposed to distributing flyers with product features.

4 HIGHER QUALITY AND MORE PRODUCTIVE SOFTWARE

Integration technology in the future will promote higher quality cost-effective solutions through more built-in quality assurance methods, and automatic collection and generation of metrics.

Functionality for testing applications will be part of the framework. All paths of the application will be tested by clicking on the test icon. Tests will be automatically generated and the results stored in the underlying database.

Version control and application builders will allow the user to choose modules from a reusable software library to create new applications. This will be a simple click and drag operation or, better still, a voice activated task. Intelligent frameworks will even create new applications from reusable parts based on the user's specification.

Creative work will still occur, but at a higher level. In fact, the user will be freed from system level commands to employ higher-level ways of communicating with the framework. This will lead to more freedom for the user to concentrate on the crucial issues in the functionality of the system, as opposed to the computer interfaces.

5 MOVING FROM TODAY

While the bulk of this article deals with technology which might occur in the future, the real fact is that there are tools in the market today which users would like to have work together, but this can be costly and time consuming.

A 1989 *Datamation* article stated that over 75 per cent of companies use tools from two or more vendors. This does not come as a surprise for many development shops. Sometimes companies themselves attempt to write code which links the various tools. More often, they have a systems integrator or a framework vendor do the work.

In some instances this integration is simply point-to-point and acts as a bridge between tools to carry information. The problem, of course, is when a newer version of a tool comes along or when the users require that additional tools be integrated.

Moving integration technology into the future, and especially toward some of the ideas discussed in this article, will require the co-operation of hardware and software vendors and systems integrators. The latter will play a key role in bringing together the best technology from different, often competitive, sources.

I believe that the role of the systems integrator is not only to link the different technologies but to promote the dialogue between the different vendors. This might be done by joint research and engineering consortia or through other forums of exchange with vendors. Actually building a framework with some of these concepts is a good way to demonstrate that many of today's enabling technologies exist; they just need to be joined.

6 CONCLUSION

Integration technology will certainly evolve and become more accessible. None of the ideas suggested in this article are exaggerated if we stop to think for a moment. The technology is progressing more rapidly than ever; it just needs to be harnessed and the right pieces put together. The challenge will be on the users, the vendors and the systems integrators to make these a reality.

Part Two

Standards and Initiatives

4 Selected Standardisation Activities Influencing CASE Integration

Kathy Chapman
Project Leader, Repository Standards, Software Development Technologies, Digital Equipment Corporation

In order to make sense of the current situation in the CASE integration standards arena, it is useful to trace the heritage of some of the key groups and their relationships with one another.

1 INTRODUCTION

The formation of the various standards groups addressing CASE integration has followed, to a certain extent, the evolution of the collective thinking in this area. One of the first problems facing those trying to automate the software engineering process was to have familiar tools available where the engineer was, i.e. on various platforms. From that problem sprang the notion of portability. Later it became clear that the engineer could be much more productive if the tools she was using co-operated. At first, and even now, tool suppliers work out agreements with each other and provide co-operating tools that way. But that is a limited and limiting approach that may be superseded at some point by data integration via a repository. Finally, it was realized that data integration via a repository, but without a common data model, is not inherently useful. So the interchange notion was given new meaning. These three aspects – portability, integrability, and interchangeability – have driven the timing and formation of several fairly autonomous consortia and *de jure* standards groups.

The European Computer Manufacturers' Association (ECMA) Technical Committee 33 (TC33) is responsible for producing the Portable Common Tool Environment (PCTE) 149 Standard, ratified in December 1990. As its title implies, its thrust is to provide an interface that is designed to support program portability by providing machine-independent access to a set of facilities.[1] However, PCTE's goal of providing an infrastructure for programs (tools) which may be part of environments supporting systems engineering projects[2] is perhaps what it is best known for today. In this context, PCTE is often referred to as a repository, but the best characterization of PCTE is as facilitator for framework development.

---

1 Standard ECMA-149, PCTE Abstract Specification, December, 1990.

2 Ibid.

During the development of the ECMA PCTE-149 Standard, the Task Group on the Reference Model (TGRM) produced the ECMA reference model that was subsequently adopted and modified by the National Institute of Standards (NIST) Integrated Software Engineering Environment (ISEE) group. NIST ISEE hopes to use the reference model to identify places where existing standards organization should place their emphasis, or where new standards organizations should be formed.

2 INTEGRABILITY

The dimensions of integrability have themselves evolved over the past four years. Data, control, and presentation integration were widely discussed at first, and only later were other dimensions, such as process, considered and addressed in standards form. Following are the definitions suggested for consideration by the X3H6 CASE Tool Integration Models committee:

- Data integration: support the management of all information in the environment as a consistent whole.
- Control integration: allow the flexible combination of an environment's functions according to project preferences and process.
- Process integration: improve the ability of tools to interact in support of a defined process.
- Presentation integration: common look and feel.
  Presentation integration has virtually always been left to groups addressing that particular problem (e.g. OSF's Motif); those working on CASE integration standardization have been concerned with data, control, and process integration.

X3H6 (CIS)

While the PCTE group was in the midst of surmounting its last obstacles on the road to ratification, a US group began forming to address the problems of CASE integration. The CASE Integration Services committee was formed in 1988 in an attempt to further data and control integration standardization activities. A Tools Integration Standard (ATIS), an object-oriented repository interface proposal jointly developed by Digital Equipment Corporation (DEC) and Atherton Technologies, Inc., was introduced into this group as a solution to the data integration problem. In 1991, the CIS group evolved into an ANSI-accredited group (X3H6, CASE Tool Integration Models) and modified its charter to include the standardization of mechanisms that allow tools to integrate with a software engineering environment. The group is building on PCTE work, and on the emerging X3H4 and CDIF work.

OMG

The Object Management Group (OMG) has become a very large organization (over 200 member companies) and has already adopted technology in its short life. The Common Object Request Broker Architecture (CORBA) was adopted in 1991, and is the underlying technology for the OMG's Object Model and Object Services. At a low level, CORBA and the Object Model and Object Services address both data and control integration.

A basic premise of the OMG's standardization process is that the technology must be commercially available for a company to submit that technology in response to an OMG RFP. This way of doing business forces the acceptance of technology to be based on current capabilities, not plans for the future. The benefit to the consumer is that the specification that is adopted is by definition implementable.

2.1 CASE communique

In 1991, HP, IBM, CDC, and Informix pooled their collective resources to form an open industry forum whose mission is to refine and standardize interfaces to HP's implementation of the Broadcast Message System (BMS) technology, SoftBench. The group's work is mostly focused on the control integration dimension.

2.2 CASE interoperability alliance

Another group of vendors, including SunSoft and DEC, began meeting with the intent to form a users group that is focusing on inter-application communication through the consensus and publication of general messages that facilitate inter-operation of independently developed networked applications"[3]. This group is planning to work through X3H6.

X3H4

During 1989, the US Information Resource Dictionary System (IRDS) group extended their list of work items to include a CASE content model and supporting interfaces. In an effort to accommodate what was sure to be a large amount of fine-grained data, the IRDS committee began considering proposals for its IRDS 2 standard. ATIS was introduced to X3H4 in the fall of 1990. The greatest stumbling block to that proposal's progression has been the reconciliation with the ISO IRDS work that is SQL-based.

---

3 CASE Interoperability Series, vol. 1, dft. 1.1.

3 INTERCHANGEABILITY

3.1 CDIF

Meanwhile, the EDIF committee began a subgroup to address CASE data interchange. Before long, that subgroup's interest area became larger than all of EDIF. CDIF became its own committee and began to quickly work towards solving the CASE data interchange problem. In the process, the group realized that exchanging meta-data, among other things, is a critical component of the whole interchange problem. Currently, the CDIF committee addresses various subject areas, and adds new ones as they become important to members.

3.2 X3H4

In October 1990, X3H4 forwarded a project proposal to the Standards Planning and Requirements Committee (SPARC) to begin standardizing the Product Data Exchange using STEP (PDES) work. This was considered to be the start of an information model project, though the SD-3 did not address the wider question at that time. In November 1991, X3H4 decided to present a CASE information model proposal to SPARC. The subcommittee was to have been numbered X3H4.5, and the base proposal was to have been IBM's AD/Cycle work. However, SPARC was forced to consider the X3H4 proposal immediately following the approval of the project that began X3H6. Therefore, SPARC sent X3H4 and X3H6 off to determine who, if anyone, should address the problem of standardizing a CASE data model.

3.3 DDSE

The committees were given six month to respond to SPARC. During that time, CDIF members became aware of, and interested in, the dilemma that faced X3H4 and X3H6. In addition, a New Work Item Proposal (NP), dated 14 July 1992, was presented to ISO/IEC JTC1 /SC7 entitled A Description of Data for Software Engineering. The purpose of the NP is to provide a means for users of software engineering tools to consistently access and interpret their descriptive data used for software engineering, to integrate that data, and to reliably exchange that data. The DDSE committee plans to do a fair amount of co-ordination among existing groups including X3H4, P1175, PDES, PCTE, and CDIF. In addition, the group plans to work on an import/export format, data flow and entity-relationship diagram descriptions, an integrated informational model, and graphical presentation.

4 SUMMARY

There are several groups addressing various aspects of the CASE integration problem. In general, the groups have disjointed membership, and this presents a co-ordination problem that groups such as the DDSE are trying to alleviate. However, there still is missing a clear road-map by which these groups can determine which direction the whole set of committees is heading and where best the contribution from the individual committees would fit.

5 GLOSSARY

- ATIS – A Tools Integration Standard
- CIA – CASE Interoperability Alliance
- CIS – CASE Integration Services committee
- CORBA – Common Object Request Broker
- DDSE – Description of Data for Software Engineering
- ECMA – European Computer Manufacturers' Association
- EDIF – Electronic Data Interchange Format
- EIA CDIF – CASE Data Interchange Format
- ISO/IEC JTC1/SC7 – The ISO/IEC /JTC1/SC7 Software Engineering is the subcommittee which covers the widest scope related to software. Its scope is as follows: development of guidelines for management techniques and standardization of supporting methods and tools necessary for the development and testing of software. SC7 membership is increasing regularly (20 primary members). It includes a special work group dealing with SC7 business planning and eight working groups. They are:
  - WG1 Symbols, Charts and Diagrams
  - WG2 System Software Documentation
  - WG4 Tools and Environment
  - WG5 Reference model for Software Development
  - WG6 Evaluation and Metrics
  - WG7 Life-Cycle Management
  - WG8 Integral Life-Cycle Process
  - WG9 Classification and Mapping
- NIST ISEE – National Institute of Standards and Technology Integrated Software Engineering Environment
- OMG – Object Management Group
- OMG OSTF – Object Management Group Object Services Task Force
- OSF – Open Systems Foundation
- PCTE – Portable Common Tool Environment
- PDES – Product Data Exchange using STEP

- P1175 – IEEE Tool-to-Tool integration standard
- SPARC – Standards Planning and Requirements Committee
- TC33 – ECMA Technical Committee 33
- TGRM – Task Group on Reference Model
- X3H4 IRDS – Information Resource Dictionary System
- X3H6 CTIM – CASE Tool Integration Models software engineering environment

5 Data Interchange between CASE Tools: PCTE, IRDS or CDIF?

Ken Thompson
The Institute of Software Engineering

1 INTRODUCTION

1.1 Background

It has been recognised for some time now that the effective use of CASE tools by a developer depends largely on the degree to which they integrate with one another. This integration involves the interchange and sharing of data as well as the ability to exchange messages and to present a common user interface style. Simply expressed, the sum of the parts can be much less than the whole for two stand-alone CASE tools but significantly greater than the whole for two integrated tools.

Developers have recognised from early experience of CASE that the data aspect of integration in particular would provide them with enormous benefits. Unfortunately, however, this is also the most difficult aspect of integration. The first step in achieving such data integration is establishing a data interchange mechanism, either via a transfer file or a shared repository according to a commonly agreed semantic model and exchange protocol.

Until recently the debate on data integration has been dominated by the activities of the major players in the software market, such as IBM with MVS/Repository Manager and to a lesser extent DEC with Cohesion/CDD+. The concentration on *de facto* standardisation activities has been at the expense of *de jure* activities by ISO and others. This was not just due to the clout of these commercial organisations but also because the *de jure* standards bodies were perceived as "not having their act together", with a multitude of unco-ordinated initiatives which clearly competed with each another.

However, in recent months this has started to change with the very significant commitment by ANSI to work more closely with ISO on these issues and the increasing level of real liaison between the different groups working under ECMA, EIA and IEEE. It seems likely, therefore, in the coming years, that the key players in the standardisation of CASE Integration will no longer be the commercial companies but rather the open standards bodies.

Open CASE Tool Integration really does seem to be coming – albeit gradually!

1.2 This paper

Against this background this report outlines the importance of, and the requirements for, CASE data interchange, which is the first step in achieving data integration. It then uses this set of requirements to review and contrast the current and likely future functionality of the three leading CASE integration standards which could claim to be truly open and *de jure* – PCTE from ECMA, IRDS from ISO and CDIF from EIA.

The paper goes on to explore different ways in which the various components of these proposed standards could fit together and co-exist in any given integration scenario. This is achieved by building up an Envelope Model of the types of data which CASE tools will have to interchange.

1.3 Acknowledgements

The author takes responsibility for all opinions and judgements expressed in this paper. The paper is a short synopsis of a full study and report of the three standands. The full study contains a complete worked example to provide an insight into the three standards.

Thanks are, however, due to Professor Dick Welke of Erasmus University in Rotterdam for his assistance in planning and reviewing early drafts.

Up-to-date information on the latest status of the on-going standards work was provided by the chairpersons of the relevant committees. Thanks are due to Mr Mike Imber, Mr David Gradwell and Mr Myer Morron for this information and guidance on its interpretation. It is not implied that they agree with all (or any) of the views expressed in the paper.

Finally thanks are due to DGXIII of the Commission of the European Communities who funded the exploratory action (ESPRIT project 25319.1/IPS) which resulted in this paper.

2 THE IMPORTANCE OF CASE DATA INTERCHANGE

2.1 Integrating CASE tools

To understand why it is necessary for CASE tools to exchange or share data it is necessary to understand the way such tools interwork. One of the most popular models for this interworking (referred to by many as the Toaster Model) is currently being expanded into a full reference model for CASE Environments (CASEEs) by both ECMA (European Computer Manufacturers' Association) in Europe and NIST (National Institute of Standards and Technology) in the US.

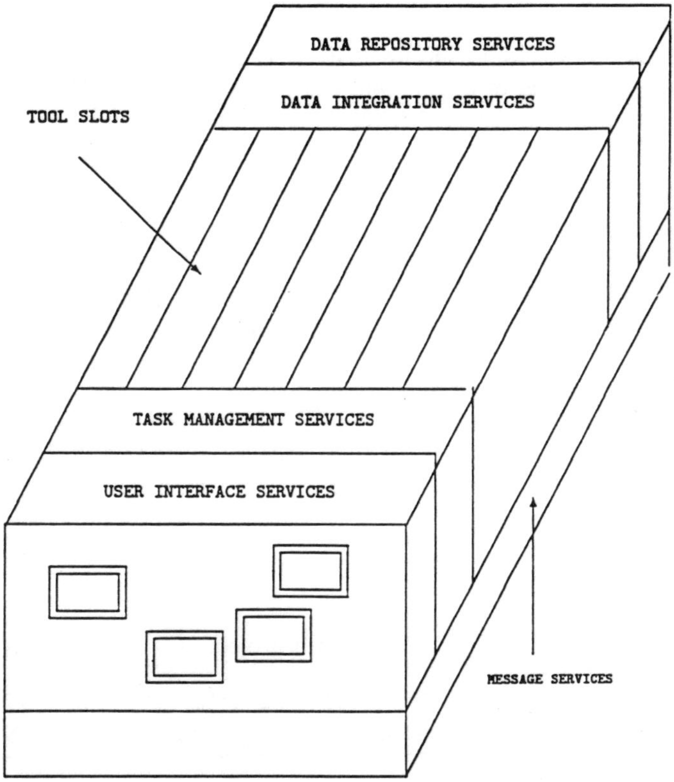

Figure 5.1 ECMA/NIST reference model for CASE environments

This model represents a CASEE as a mechanism with slots into which CASE tools plug. Each tool must work with the CASEE in three main ways. Firstly it must allow the CASEEs' Data Integration Services to manage any of its data which needs to be accessed by other tools. The CASEE Data Integration Services are responsible for controlling the access to, and integrity of, this data but not for its storage – it delegates this to the CASEE Data Repository Services.

The second way that the CASE tool must co-operate with the CASEE is to use its Task Management Services wherever it needs to communicate with any other CASE tool using the CASEE. The type of information that would be passed is control information such as Task Completed. Such information could then allow a development scheduling tool to invoke another tool with a particular set of parameters to progress the overall process which the first tool was working on. Hence the managing of this type of information is referred to as Control or Process Integration. The actual passing of messages between tools is delegated to the CASEE Message Services component.

The final way that a CASE tool must work with the CASEE is to use its User Interface Services to ensure that all user interaction is performed in a similar way. Provision of a common look and feel between CASE tools makes it easier for a user to move between them – this is known as Presentation Integration.

2.2 The reasons for data interchange

These three types of CASE tool integration become crucial to isolated CASE tools whenever they wish to communicate with other tools. This paper concentrates on data integration because it is not only the area of biggest potential benefit but also the most problematic.

There are many reasons why a CASE tool would want to communicate its data to another tool. The most common reasons are shown in the Figure 5.2.

Reason	Frequency	Directions
Migration	one-off	1-way
Automation	throughout a project	1-way*
Reverse Engineering	throughout a project	1-way*
Control	throughout a project	1-way*
Co-operation	throughout a project phase	2-way

* mainly 1-way but with an occasional need to go other way, either programmatically or manually, to keep data consistent.

Figure 5.2 Reasons for CASE data interchange

The above examples of the many reasons for wanting data interchange between CASE tools highlight the potentially large benefits if such interchange can be successfully achieved. However it is not easy!

2.3 The difficulties with data interchange

There are two main problems in exchanging data between CASE tools – establishing a protocol and agreeing on the meaning of the data to be exchanged. If we imagine two European scientists attempting to converse about physics at a distance then the issue of the telecommunications medium (e.g. phone) and the language to be used (e.g. English) are protocol issues. The issue of the exact meaning of the terms used (e.g. Oxford Dictionary of Science) is a data meaning or semantics issue.

The problem of transfer protocol is the simpler of the two problems but is by no means trivial. A transfer protocol is necessary because CASE tools will be running on different real systems, operating environments, and will be storing their data in their own optimised internal file representations. The tools may provide the means of exporting their data from this internal format into, say, a more accessible ASCII file format. However this format will also be proprietary to the CASE tool developer. There are currently no non-proprietary transfer protocols which have been widely implemented.

The problem of preserving meaning is much more serious. Each CASE tool tends to embody its own proprietary interpretation of the data necessary to build software systems. Modern good practices of software engineering employ a number of techniques based around various graphical diagrams. These diagrams are generally based around a small number of diagram types such as tables, structured text, graphs and trees. However, the cursory similarity of such diagrams hides a wealth of different meaning and, conversely, the dissimilarity of certain diagram types hides a great degree of common meaning!

For example CASE Tool 1 will model the occurrence of a particular object as a Data Entity whilst CASE Tool 2 will model the same object as a Data Relationship which only exists as a link between Data Entities. CASE Tool 1 will use the term Function in a systems planning study as a high-level business-oriented operation conducted by an enterprise. CASE Tool 2 will use the term Function as the lowest level of program code grouping during detailed systems design. There is no question of right and wrong – both are right in the context of their intended usage!

If we compare the data semantics of CASE Tool 1 and CASE Tool 2 we can classify the degree of correspondence between each semantic construct into one of three partitions. A Direct Match occurs where the semantics of two constructs fully agree – in this case data transfer is easy. A Transformable Match occurs where the semantics of two constructs are similar enough to allow a mapping to be defined between the two. Such a match can be simple, i.e. a complete two-way mapping. In other cases it may be complex, leading to incomplete and one-way only mappings. Much of the CASE tool data which developers are interested in transferring falls into the Transformable Match partition. This is responsible for a large number of the problems encountered in CASE tool data interchange today.

The final partition between CASE Tool 1 and CASE Tool 2 is the No Match category. In this category one of the tools is either collecting data or associating it in some manner which is neither the same as nor even similar to, anything in the other tool. Thus CASE Tool 1 cannot hope to have even a good approximation of such data populated by CASE Tool 2. This can cause severe problems in data interchange, especially if CASE Tool 1 considers such information to be mandatory and will not allow originating records from CASE Tool 2 even to be saved in its own file representation without this information.

Now, if only a very small number of CASE tools existed then the above difficulties could be largely overcome by the provision of a few well-tried point-to-point interfaces between each tool. Today's difficulty is that the number of tools is large and growing. We are not even able to say we will restrict transfer to tools within the same part of the software life-cycle, as we have seen earlier that the many reasons for interchange force both inter and intra life-cycle phase transfers. It is easily calculated that the number of point-point interfaces rises as N(N-1) where N is the number of tools. Thus point-point interfaces between more than a handful of tools are simply impractical to develop and maintain.

Due to the above problems CASE data interchange is both inefficient and ineffective. At best only a small percentage of required data is interchanged successfully. Existing interfaces tend to be *ad hoc*, work on the 80-20 rule (i.e. does just 80 per cent of the job), depend heavily on human intervention (for the other 20 per cent) and are seldom two-way! Many users, having experienced the problems of using such interfaces, have resorted to rekeying the data by hand. Unfortunately the manual process has to deal with all the same problems plus the added one of human inconsistency!

3 MECHANISMS FOR CASE DATA INTERCHANGE

3.1 Data Interchange Mechanisms (DIMs)

There are essentially two ways to interchange data between CASE tools – either by the exchange data being stored in an intermediate transfer file or in a database. When an intermediate transfer file is used it is sometimes referred to as a DIF (Data Interchange File). When a database is used to store software engineering data it is called a data dictionary or repository. The database approach has two variants. Either the sending tool can write directly to the repository (using a Services Interface) or it can create a transfer file (Import/Export) in a format suitable for processing against the repository. We call these three approaches Language Only, Repository Direct Access and Repository With Language respectively.

In the paper we have used the term Data Interchange Mechanism (DIM) to refer collectively to all three approaches. The relationship between a DIM and the file-based (DIF) and repository-based approaches is shown in Figure 5.3. In essence the DIM is only concerned with repository functionality to assist in *ad hoc* (single-user) data transformations of interchanged data. The important issues concerning controlling multi-user access to the data such as locking, deadlock and serialisability, are outside the scope of the DIM.

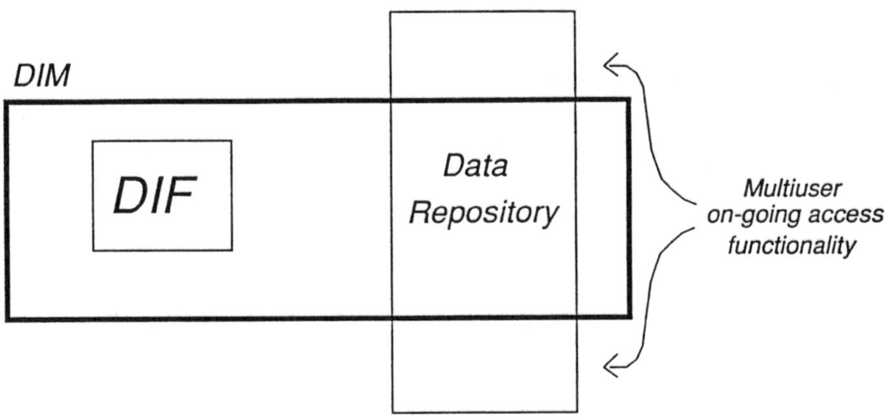

Figure 5.3 Relationship between DIM, DIF and data repository

We therefore define a DIM as follows:

A CASE Data Interchange Mechanism allows the efficient and open transfer of data between software engineering tools with minimum loss.

Concerning the efficient aspect of a DIM, we are primarily interested in whether the DIM has the means of storing the information to be transferred. A second important consideration, however, given the earlier discussion regarding the need for data transformation, is whether the DIM provides a means of manipulating this data to an extent. Generally only a DIM based around a repository will provide the latter capabilities.

The open aspect of the definition means, firstly, that the specification of the DIM must be publicly available. More importantly, it also means that the management of its evolution must be under the control of a recognised international standards body.

Minimum loss also has two aspects to it. Firstly, there must be data structures within the DIM of the right meaning, type and size to store the particular items of CASE data needing to be transferred. Secondly, those data structures should provide no loss storage. By no loss we mean storage which does not semantically change or deplete the information.

Thus given a total no loss representation a CASE tool could create a DIM export file, empty its own data dictionary and then, by importing the same file, automatically reconstruct the data and its pictorial representation exactly in its original form. Given the previous examples, it can be seen that it is unlikely that any DIM could provide a total no loss transfer capability to any CASE tool – hence the term Minimum Loss.

3.2 International standards

In this paper we have considered three emerging (potentially) international standards which satisfy many of the requirements specified for a DIM above.

The first standard is CDIF (CASE Data Interchange Format) which has progressed to a trial-use standard under the US EIA (Electronic Industries Association). CDIF is a Language Only data integration mechanism.

The second standard is ISO IRDS (Information Resource Dictionary System) which has progressed to international standard for its framework document and to draft international standard for its services interface. IRDS is currently a Repository Direct Access DIM. The IRDS work conducted under ANSI is outside the scope of this paper.

The third standard is PCTE (Portable Common Tools Environment) which has progressed to an ECMA (European Computer Manufacturers' Association) standard for its abstract specification and the C language binding of its services interface. PCTE is also a Repository Direct Access DIM.

It must be noted that of the three only CDIF set out with the design objective of being a DIM. IRDS is a standardisation of a CASE data dictionary or repository. PCTE was originally the standardisation of an IPSE (Integrated Project Support Environment) developed for LowerCASE technical software development tools. More recently it has evolved into the CASEE (CASE Environment) area also covering the repository.

3.3 Meta-data and four-level architectures

Before we begin to outline the components of a Data Interchange Mechanism we need to understand the different levels of CASE data it must handle.

In discussing database applications we distinguish between types of data such as CUSTOMER or ORDER and instances of such data like ACME Ltd and 12309. We have the same situation in CASE tools but with types such as ENTITY and PROCESS, and with instances like CUSTOMER and Place Order. We can see immediately that what a CASE user calls instances are actually types from an applications user's perspective. Thus CASE overlaps the application domain and adds a further higher level of abstraction.

This higher level of abstraction is known as the Meta-Data Layer and models described with it as meta models. In the meta model we define the rules for each of the techniques being used in the CASE tool. Each CASE tool has either an implicit or explicit meta model (expressed using a form of Entity-Relationship modelling) which controls the data it captures in supporting various CASE techniques.

As well as the meta-data layer CASE tools have a further level of internal abstraction known as the Meta-Meta-Data Layer or Meta-Meta Model. The need for a meta-meta model becomes obvious whenever we begin to construct meta models. Before we can document such models we need to decide on a syntactical and semantic notation. Such a notation (again implicit or explicit) is a meta-meta model and like the meta model, is expressed using Entity-Relationship modelling.

To help in the understanding of these concepts the idea of a four-level architecture of CASE data is often used. All three of the standards adopt such an architecture but they name each of the levels in a different way, as shown in Figure 5.4 along with a typical instance of each data level.

Typical Instance	CDIF	IRDS	PCTE
OBJECT	Meta-Meta	Fundamental	Meta Schema
ENTITY	Meta	IRD Defn.	Schema Defn.
CUSTOMER	Model	IRD	Object
ACME Ltd	Application	Application	(Undefined)

Figure 5.4 Names for the four data levels

Throughout this paper we will use the CDIF names for the four levels as they seem to be the clearest and most universally understood. Note also that none of the mechanisms permit transfer or storage of Application Data – this is the responsibility of the Application Database. It is worth noting, however, that an application database does not just contain application data: it also must contain model data in the form of definitions of schemas for the data it contains. Thus a database which stores employee details must also store the types (e.g. Table Employee containing Column Employee Number) of which these employee details are the instances.

3.4 Components of a data interchange mechanism

A Data Interchange Mechanism can be considered as having up to five major components, as shown in Figure 5.5.

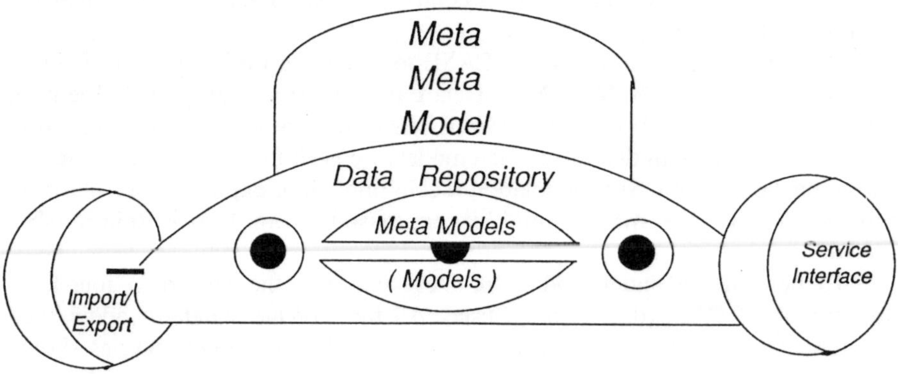

Figure 5.5 Five components of a data interchange mechanism

A meta-meta model controls the constructs which may be used in meta models and is generally immutable. A meta model describes the techniques a CASE tool can support along with their rules. An Import/Export Language provides a means of bulk loading the data in a CASE tool into the DIM. It also allows the DIM to write an intermediate file for a CASE tool. A Repository Services Interface is a means for a program to access the Data Repository directly without creating an intermediate Import/Export File. Finally the data repository is the database which holds CASE model data and its meta data.

We have drawn the figure like a racing car to illustrate that we can consider the model data to be the petrol and the meta model Data the water. Without both of these the DIM will not run!

4 AN ENVELOPE MODEL OF CASE DATA INTERCHANGE

4.1 The types of CASE data

To successfully interchange CASE data we need to understand how it is composed. If we were to look at the data inside a CASE tool we might find both meta model and model data. Generally we are interested in the transfer of model data only, which we can divide it into three categories – semantic data, presentation data and management control data.

It is, however, possible and desirable to be able to transfer varying degrees of meta data. At the simplest level, a CASE tool vendor might wish to record which version of a publicly available meta model it was using in its transfer file. At a more complex level, two CASE tool vendors who, by private agreement, wished to add a semantic construct to a public meta model might choose to prefix any transfer file with the specification of this additional construct. (For ultimate flexibility in transfer of data a CASE tool would also need to describe the notation used in such a meta model i.e. its meta-meta model. For the remainder of this report we will concentrate on the transfer of model data only.)

The first component of model data is Semantic Data which could, for example, contain details of processes and stores in a data flow diagram. Presentation Data might give the grid co-ordinates, shapes and sizes of these objects on the diagram. Management Control Data might define who created each of the objects and which project they belong to.

Once this data leaves the CASE tool it needs to have a fourth category of data added to it to enable it to communicate with another tool. This Environmental Control Data might specify the transfer syntax, the encoding used and the character set of the data. We can represent the six categories of CASE data as shown in Figure 5.6, with each outer layer enveloping each inner layer. The meta-meta and meta-data layers are shown for completeness only.

It would be interesting to expand this idea further and compare it with ISO standards like ODA/ODIF (IS8613) for open document interchange to see if it could provide foundation concepts for a generalised model for the definition and exchange of any data.

It is of fundamental importance in considering the usefulness of a Data Interchange Mechanism that we consider its ability to store and manipulate at least the three innermost categories of CASE data. A DIM which cannot transfer presentation data will not allow the successful transfer of carefully laid out diagrams without human reworking. A DIM which cannot transfer management control data will likewise lose important information.

We will now look at each category of CASE data in more detail.

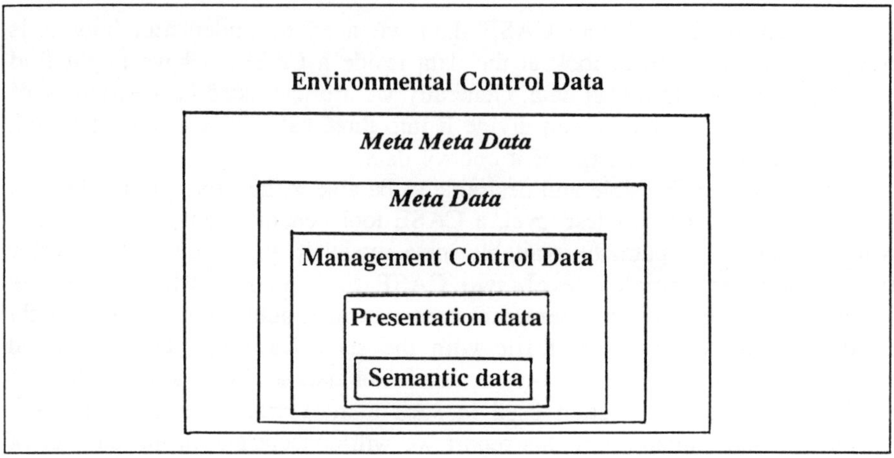

Figure 5.6 An envelope model of CASE data

4.2 Semantic data

There are three key issues to be considered in the semantic data – rules for naming and uniqueness of objects in models, the technique coverage and the level of granularity of objects.

The meta model should place no constraints upon the naming and identity of objects in CASE models as this is CASE tool/methodology dependent. For example, in some CASE tools object instance names must be unique across all object types whilst others may enforce uniqueness within an object type. It should also allow for identification of objects, if required, through a concatenation of a number of fields.

Data held in CASE tools is mostly held in the context of a particular technique or set of techniques. Thus, rather than transfer all the data from one CASE tool to another we would more likely want to transfer, say, all the Data Flow Diagrams, then all the Entity Relationship Diagrams and so on. A transfer of data held according to a particular software engineering technique can only take place when two tools are in agreement as to the nature of this data. In other words the tools must be working to a mutually agreed meta model which acts as a superset of their implementations of the particular technique. Thus transfer between tools can only take place when a meta model exists which supersets the required techniques.

A vast number of techniques currently exist for all stages in the software engineering life cycle. Also different techniques are relevant at similar stages of the life cycle depending on whether the system is a real-time system or an Information System. For example an IS system might require Entity-Relationship modelling followed by Data-Flow modelling, whilst the same stage of development of a real-time system might require Data-Flow modelling with real-time extensions followed by State-Transition modelling.

Even when we agree upon a technique we will probably find very different interpretations of the precise semantics of the technique. For example Figure 5.7 lists some of the constructs which cause dispute between techniques in the single area of entity-relationship diagraming.

• How many Entities can a Relationship connect?
• Can Relationships have Attributes?
• Are Many-to-Many Relationships Permitted?
• Is Sub-Typing Permitted?
• Can Relationships be exclusive?
• Do Relationships have one name or two?
• Can Entities be complex?
• What are the allowed Entity types?
• What are the allowed Relationship types?
• Can Attributes be shared between Entities ?
• How is Relationship cardinality and optionality shown?
• Are Roles Supported?
Constraints, Domains, Validation Rules, Keys.....etc.

Figure 5.7 Different constructs of E-R modelling

A key aspect, therefore, of the evaluation of a DIM is the question, Does its meta model effectively cover the major techniques being used in the CASE tools it aims to interconnect?

The second key issue about CASE semantic data is its **granularity**, or in other words how many objects (records) are required to fully represent it. For example, a Process Decomposition Diagram is an example of a technique resulting in a number of small objects representing processes and their decompositions. Each of these objects only has a small amount of inherent properties which need recording. Therefore these are multiple **fine-grained objects with low content**. However, if we look at a process specification in pseudo-code of a COBOL module then we might consider this to be a single object with a large amount of properties to represent each line of specification i.e. a single **coarse-grained object with high content.**

Until quite recently the generalisation that UpperCASE techniques mostly resulted in fine-granularity objects and LowerCASE mostly resulted in coarse-granularity objects seemed to be quite valid. However, one of the major innovations in recent years, and one of the main reasons for integrating CASE tools, is to transform the output of one tool into the input of another. The existence of coarse-granularity objects at advanced stages in the life cycle limits our ability to effectively associate them with fine-grain objects from which they are derived. This is because implicit objects (such as a line of code), which are hidden within the content of coarse-grain objects, are not easily or efficiently manipulated.

This means that we must carefully assess both the meta model and the underlying data repository architecture of the DIM for its strategy for storage of both fine-grained and coarse-grained objects.

4.3 Presentation data

Each semantic object stored in a CASE tool has a pictorial representation for each diagram it appears on. It is desirable that this representation is as accurately preserved as possible in any information transfer between tools. One of the main problems currently in achieving this objective is that most of the present generation of CASE tools are fairly inflexible in what they can represent. This current lack of technology should not be allowed to lock us into a DIM which may constrain us in the future as a number of tools (Meta-CASE) are emerging with much more flexibility of both semantics and presentation.

There is however a counter argument to the above which suggests that excess care spent in presentation layout is time wasted. Supporters of this view suggest that the future generation of graphical CASE tools will simply ask us to identify the main objects in a diagram and then it will intelligently cluster the rest around these. It is important therefore that a DIM neither forces the capture of excessive presentation information nor inhibits it.

It seems possible to identify a number of levels of presentation-information capture to simplify the evaluation of a DIM, as shown in Figure 5.8.

At level one we are simply transferring location information, whereas from level two upwards we are beginning to allow individual objects to be redefined in terms of shape, extent, orientation etc. It should be noted also that presentation information for all types of diagrams needs to be transferred. This includes graphs, trees, tables and structured text.

Level	Description	Importer Responsibilities
0	No presentation data	Presentation inferred from semantic data
1	X:Y Co-ords and size	Importer decides shapes and link representation
2	Object shapes	Shape and link representation processed
3	Meta presentation	Importer reproduces diagram – many levels!

Figure 5.8 Levels of presentation data

4.4 Management control data

This type of data can be divided into a number of aspects:

Partitions	Overlapping (e.g. Projects) and non-overlapping (Stages)
Versions	Version Trees and Graphs
Audit Information	Object Modification Details/History
Access and Security	Discretionary and Mandatory Security
Configurations	Versionable Complex Objects
Integrity	Constraints, Book-in/Book-out...

4.5 Environmental Control Data

This type of data can also be divided into a number of aspects:

Transfer Syntaxes	e.g. ASN.1* compliance, existing objects...
Syntax Encodings	e.g. Textual, Binary, Compact...
Character Sets	e.g. ASCII, EBCDIC

*ASN.1 (Abstract Syntax Notation Number 1) is an OSI Presentation Layer specification used by X.400 (Electronic Mail and Messaging). It is a syntax notation language used to formally define network protocols and is ISO standard 8824/8825.

5 PCTE, IRDS AND CDIF COMPARED – BY COMPONENT

5.1 Overview

An outline comparison of each of the standards against each of the components is as shown in Figure 5.9:

	CDIF	IRDS	PCTE
A Meta-Meta Model	Yes	Yes	Yes
A Meta Model	Partial*	RDBMS Design	Vendors
An Import/Export Language	Yes	No	No
A Data Repository	No	Yes	Yes
A Repository Services Interface	No	Yes	Yes

* Only data modelling and process modelling currently.

Figure 5.9 Standards by DIM component

It will be noted immediately that none of the standards offer components necessary to provide all the functions required by a DIM. It needs to be possible therefore to mix and match to varying degrees between the components of the different standards. This is not as difficult as it sounds and has already been achieved in small degrees. For example, a prototype IRDS Services Interface has been built which uses the PCTE OMS as its data repository. More importantly IRDS does not plan to invent all its own meta models aspect but instead to adapt other work in the area where appropriate, such as the meta models developed by CDIF.

5.2 Meta-meta models

All three standards have an explicitly defined meta-meta model. All three essentially provide variations of binary ERA modelling. IRDS provides this by using SQL2 Data Definition Language with the integrity addendum – hence entities are modelled as tables, attributes as columns with relationships modelled via constraints. Both CDIF and PCTE allow single and multiple inheritance of attributes and relationships. IRDS does not directly support inheritance, using instead 1:1 exclusive relationships. However, it is possible that the services interface (which is now a draft international standard) may be modified to support the SQL3 concept of subtables which would allow both single and multiple inheritance. IRDS does not support Attributed Relationships and Many-to-Many Relationships unlike both CDIF and IRDS.

The major unique of the IRDS meta-meta model is that its use of SQL2 provides it with a very powerful constraint specification language. The major unique of PCTE is that it allows a core meta model (known as a Schema Description Set) to be inherited and locally altered, for example by adding new attributes. This can ease extensibility as changes can often be restricted to local views without wider impact. IRDS could emulate this to a certain extent by setting up views of a meta model, although they would not be extensible like PCTE. CDIF's major unique is probably its elegant simplicity in that it only contains five constructs.

None of the meta-meta models allow for N-Ary relationships, unlike some other proprietary meta-modelling techniques (e.g. Object Property Role Relationship or NIAM). It is important to understand that this does not inhibit such constructs appearing in interchange data but only in meta models. The ability to use these constructs in meta models can improve conciseness of representation, reduce the chance of information loss, and thus can improve the efficiency and integrity of transfer.

5.3 Meta models

Neither IRDS nor PCTE has yet attempted major standardisation of meta models. IRDS has so far only addressed Design Support for SQL in draft whereas PCTE has left the meta model aspect to implementors as added-value dimensions. Both IRDS and PCTE seem to see their role as providing suitable containers for meta models originated by others. Thus only CDIF provides any direct coverage of the meta model.

The CDIF meta model currently covers part of the UpperCASE area with ERA models being covered by two subject areas (Entity Relationship and Data Inventory) and DFD modelling by another. These models have been circulated widely over the CASE tool vendor and user community over the last eighteen months and it seems likely that they now represent a reasonable first-cut superset of the vast majority of the constructs needed. Extensions which will be required include Object-Oriented Analysis and Real-Time extensions to DFDs.

Thus CDIF covers an important aspect of software development i.e. a subset of analysis and design techniques in depth. However, it currently only covers a fraction of the software life cycle with the following as yet unsupported:

- Real-Time Extensions to DFDs
- Object-Oriented Analysis and Design
- Database Design for RDBMS, Hierarchical DBMS and Indexed Files
- Screen Design of block mode, character mode and bit-mapped/GUI interfaces
- Program Design including Program Structure and Pseudo Code
- Transaction Analysis and Design
- Distributed Design using Distributed Databases and Co-operative Processing
- Project Management and Metrics
- Information Strategy Planning

Figure 5.10 Future meta model areas

It is CDIF's intention, however, that work should commence in a number of the above areas. For example, working papers exist for State-Transition Diagrams.

5.4 Import/export languages

Neither IRDS nor PCTE has an import/export language. Both groups are in discussions with CDIF regarding the possibility of adapting its exchange syntax to act a import/export into their data repositories.

PCTE report that CDIF representatives have attended the last two PCTE ECMA meetings (TC33) with further liaison planned in the Autumn. CDIF also reported that they have become involved in the US/European PCIS Workshops which are defining the requirements for a version of PCTE for both civil and military use. Less formal discussions between CDIF and IRDS are also taking place regarding import/export. Here the mechanism for talks is more convoluted, with EIA having to route discussions to ISO via ANSI.

It must be noted however that the CDIF work will not just plug in to the other standards unchanged – it will be adapted rather than adopted! For example, the CDIF Import/Export Syntax was developed for a given meta model (and meta-meta model) and repository component (i.e. none). Thus to use a CDIF Transfer with, say, IRDS it would be necessary to split many-to-many clauses (which IRDS does not support) and to build in statements to the transfer file to allow for roll-back and recovery and the referencing of existing repository objects. Some of these changes will be minor and could be accommodated by filtering a CDIF transfer file, whilst others will be very much more significant.

CDIF currently offers a single human-readable LISP-like syntax which permits transfer of changes to a base meta model as well as transferring model data. CDIF also plan to produce an ASN.1 compliant syntax (ASN.1 is the ISO standard for Abstract Syntax Notation), a condensed syntax and possibly an STL syntax (STL is the import/export syntax proposed by the IEEE Task Force for Professional Tools). A fully worked example of CDIF syntax is contained in the full report.

5.5 Data repositories

CDIF does not have a data repository. Both PCTE and IRDS provide a repository for the management of both CASE data and meta-data – but not of course application data. Both PCTE and IRDS aim to be independent of any underlying database architecture. Thus IRDS states that the use of SQL as a definition formalism does not imply any specific implementation approach. A complete example of the tables necessary to describe meta models (IRD Definition) and models (IRD) is contained in the full report.

The PCTE Object Management System (OMS) can also be implemented either over an operating system's filestore or over a database or file management system such as an RDBMS. For reasons of efficiency it seems that OMS implementations have been predominantly over filestores within UNIX and VMS with replacement of the hierarchical structure with a network of bidirectional links. The file contents are then used for storing fine-grain data and the file attributes are generalised to give further information about the objects.

Storage of fine-grain objects as file contents gives rise to problems as standardisation of file contents is outside the scope of PCTE. This has led to it having to be addressed as an added-value activity by PCTE tool builders like IPSYS who have implemented a two-tier structure with a common services interface to effectively handle fine-grain data.

5.6 Repository services interfaces

CDIF not having a data repository does not have a repository services interface. IRDS attempts to provide a core of Level-Independent Services which can operate both at meta model (IRD definition) and model (IRD) level. It also provides a set of Operational Services to initiate and terminate processing and to initiate and terminate transactions. The final set of services are termed IRD Definition Level Services and are used to create, drop, reactivate or deactivate an IRD, or to validate an IRD Schema Group. All access to the repository is via these services which maintain integrity and enforce any required constraints.

PCTE provides a comprehensive set of services for accessing, updating and creating objects, their attributes, their contents and links. It also provides built-in services for managing versions, configurations and security. It does not, however, attempt to provide Level-Independent Services which can operate on both data and meta-data. Thus there are separate services, OBJECT_CREATE and SDS_CREATE_OBJECT_TYPE. A complete example showing how PCTE would define and populate an SDS is contained in the full report.

At present no concrete language bindings exist for the IRDS services which are described in an abstract manner using ISO Pascal. PCTE has C-Language binding as well as the abstract specification. An ADA binding is also available in draft and likely to be approved by the end of 1991.

6 PCTE, IRDS AND CDIF COMPARED – BY THE ENVELOPE MODEL

6.1 Overview

We will now outline to what extent each of the three standards provide the mechanisms to transfer CASE data according to the layers of the Envelope Model shown in Figure 5.6. We will focus on the three data levels – Semantic, Presentation, and Management Control.

6.2 Semantic data

This has already been outlined in **5.3.**

6.3 Presentation data

As CDIF is the only standard of the three addressing meta models only it addresses presentation information. There is, however, no inherent reason why either IRDS or PCTE could not make use of presentation information contained in resident meta models.

CDIF provides an extensive, but untried, meta model section for specifying model presentation information. It splits into two sections, one describing the definitions of presentation objects and the other describing specific instances of presentation objects. There is a link between the definition part of the presentation meta model and the semantic meta model to link visualisation and meaning. The definition link would show for example that an Entity is a Rectangle. It recognises Nodes (such as Entity boxes) and Edges (such as Relationship lines), each of which can be complimented with various visual aspects (such as Names, Arrows ect.).

It appears to be extremely comprehensive and allows for the capture of nearly all of the graphical constructs currently used in the UpperCASE tool diagrams which CDIF supports. This is an important point as the model will need to be carefully reviewed as support for techniques using diagram types (such as tables and matrices) which are not based on nodes and links are added.

6.4 Management control data

In general, given the limited coverage of its meta model, CDIF is much more limited in this area than both PCTE and IRDS. However, given CDIF's public and private extensibility mechanisms, it should be possible for a CASE tool vendor to extend the model to add specific management control data where required. In the case of both PCTE and IRDS many of the following facilities are built in to the meta-meta model and are therefore not intended to be extensible.

Partitioning

IRDS groups objects (at both meta model and model level) into Working Sets. An object can exist in only one working set but can have read-only access objects in other working sets.

PCTE can group objects into configurations known as complex objects which behave in all respects as atomic objects. An atomic object can be shared between more than one configuration provided its exclusiveness property is set to shared.

CDIF provides facilities to group data model and process model objects together and to provide multiple views of them. It does not provide a higher level project grouping. It does however allow each object to be assigned to a life-cycle phase and can record the relationships between these phases.

Version management

IRDS applies versioning at the working set level. Therefore to access a particular version you specify its name and your context indicates the working set name and version. A working set can be based on another single working set (i.e. tree structure) and can reference a number of working sets. Each working set has an attribute IRD_CONTENT_STATUS which indicates whether it is accepting updates directly or indirectly through the propagation of an update from a working set it is based on. working sets can also be merged. IRDS applies no constraints to version naming schemes.

PCTE provides versioning at object level, supporting a directed acyclic graph which allows for versions to depend on more than one predecessor provided no circularity occurs. PCTE provides two basic in-built versioning operations, Snapshot and Revise. Both create copies of objects (atomic or complex), the only difference being that with Snapshot the new object is the predecessor of the original object, and with Revise the new object is the successor of the original object. In both cases the predecessor cannot be changed – i.e. unlike IRDS old object versions are immutable once a new version is created.

CDIF provides no versioning cover within its current meta model.

Audit information

All three standards provide auditing information, with CDIF and IRDS considering it as properties of the object, and PCTE holding it as a separate change log.

IRDS holds an audit attribute against each object version showing name and time stamp of creation, update and the number of times modified.

PCTE maintains a separate audit file which is written to on all user-defined critical events.

CDIF can hold create, update and responsibility name and time stamps against each object, property and relationship. It does not however keep an history of updates.

Access and security

CDIF currently offers nothing in the access and security area other than the Responsibility flag at object level.

IRDS offers discretionary security facilities but no mandatory security facilities. Access is controlled at working set level based on the select, insert, delete and update privilege granted to the particular user by another user (the grantor). IRDS does not support user groups.

PCTE offers both comprehensive discretionary and mandatory security facilities at object level which support users and user groups. Mandatory security is implemented by associating two labels with each object – a Confidentiality label to prevent unauthorised disclosure and an Integrity label to prevent contribution to the object from unauthorised sources.

Configuration management

CDIF could support complex entities through its Cluster meta entity in the core subject area which can group together entities and relationships.

IRDS implements configurations at meta-meta model level through references from a working set to others which may in turn reference other working sets. In this way it provides a means for the IRDS user to reference, as a single unit, a collection of object versions of various object types whose content is controlled by some other IRDS user.

PCTE also implements configurations at meta-meta model level but as complex objects consisting of a root component and all those other objects joined to it via composition links. Atomic objects can be shared between more than one configuration. Configurations of objects in PCTE behave like atomic objects in respect of all PCTE services.

Integrity

In a tightly controlled repository we could say that the data must always be consistent with the rules specified in the meta model. However a DIM has to transfer data between different CASE tools, each of which may have a radically different policy on integrity. For example, CASE Tool 1 may allow the capture of both incomplete and incorrect information errors which are reported on by batch reports. CASE Tool 2, however, may not allow such data to be saved in its internal repository. How then do we transfer data from CASE Tool 1 to 2? Firstly we must apply common sense and never knowingly transfer dubious data. However, even after passing CASE Tool 1's batch checks, the data may still be invalid according to CASE Tool 2.

We therefore need the ability for the DIM either to turn integrity on or off or to have some constraints mandatory and others optional. If the DIM opts for the integrity on/off approach, controls must exist to ensure unchecked data is not used as the basis for any other data until it is fixed.

CDIF provides no mechanisms for managing integrity. It is possible to create a transfer file which is inconsistent with the CDIF meta model. It is the responsibility of the importing tool to detect and handle such problems.

IRDS allows both optional and mandatory integrity constraints, the latter always enforced. A deactivate/reactivate service is provided to allow changes to be made to an IRD Definition which has existing IRD data stored. Once these changes are validated the IRD may be reactivated. If any inconsistencies have arisen between the IRD and its definition then the reactivate service would fail and return an error code.

PCTE implements referential integrity through Existence and Reference Link Types. It also supports transaction locking and roll-back.

7 CONCLUSIONS

7.1 Summary

We have to conclude that at this point in time data interchange between CASE tools using either of the three standards is not yet possible. It is imminent however, with CDIF currently undergoing a prototyping phase where CASE tool developers are building interfaces according to the trial-use standard to validate and refine the meta models and exchange syntax.

However, even on the successful completion of this exercise, CDIF will only allow the semantics and presentation of UpperCASE techniques to be interchanged. It will also not cover the management control layer of CASE data containing such information as versions and partitions. Without such control information, data integration (data sharing) as opposed to interchange would be very difficult to achieve.

Data integration also, of course, needs a data repository. It seems therefore that the most likely scenario for integration via these three standards will emerge in two to three years. By this point it is likely that CDIF will form the basis for import/export into at least one of the two other repository-based initiatives, PCTE or IRDS. If by this point open meta model coverage of the management control data aspects has become more substantial then these standards will provide the basis for successful data integration.

Another key milestone in data integration especially important for CASE IS developers is the provision of meta model coverage for process specifications, user interface layouts and database design. Without these the integration mechanisms will not be able to support the growing trend for automated application generation and maintenance from analysis and design information.

Real-time developers have the more immediate problem of ensuring that the analysis and design techniques do not just cover IS but also their requirements. These include the real-time extensions to data-flow diagrams, the provision of state-transition diagrams and object-oriented analysis and design constructs.

7.2 Actions for the CASE user

Although it is too early to achieve data interchange using PCTE, IRDS and CDIF it is certainly not too early to start commencing preparation work. In fact, assuming that CDIF data interchange becomes possible during 1992 the user organisation that starts now should be well on the way to being able to intercept the CDIF into PCTE or IRDS scenario two to three years from now, which would enable real data integration.

So what should a user organisation do? Firstly, it should ensure that the introduction of interchange and integration technology is, like any other CASE investment, based on sound business and not just technological reasons. Experience to date has shown that one of the critical success factors in the successful introduction of CASE technology has been whether an organisation adopted a strategic as opposed to an *ad hoc* approach to its implementation.

CASE data interchange/integration strategies cannot however be defined in isolation. They need to be defined in the context of an overall CASE strategy. This is because the overall effectiveness of a CASE portfolio depends on two related factors, the (stand-alone) effectiveness of the tools plus their degree of integration. Thus an initial list of ideal CASE tools may need to be revised due to poor integration potential, and excellent integration schemes may need to be discarded due to poor tool support!

Other important CASE user actions include:

- assessing the degree of proprietary (closed) integration already present in the organization's existing CASE tools;
- defining the objectives for integration (see Figure 5.2);
- following the progress and plans of the integration standards (both *de facto* and *de jure*) activities, and in particular the on-going IRDS v. PCTE debate;

- monitoring CASE vendors integration strategies and tangible commitment to implement open standards.

7.3 Actions for the CASE vendor

As outlined above, CASE tool developers need to publish their current capabilities and future strategies with respect to integration standards. Furthermore, they need to provide more detailed and less vague compliance information than has been the case in the past.

More CASE tool developers need to participate in the evolution of meta models – an enormously difficult and time-consuming activity! So far the 80/20 rule seems to have applied with 80 per cent of the CASE vendors nodding approval at work conducted by the other 20 per cent. However, meta model development for new subject areas is a complex and resource-consuming business and the resource being consumed is usually the most senior technical staff within the company. There has also been a tendency for some vendors not to be as open with their meta models as they might have been, for no good business reason.

Without more widespread participation there is a serious threat that existing meta models will stagnate as the companies in the 20 per cent struggle to resource the on-going evolution.

7.4 Hopes for the standards activities

It is hoped that the standards bodies will continue the dialogues they have started to reduce unnecessary duplication of efforts which restricts users' integration options. It also wastes an already scarce resource which in terms of CDIF, IRDS and PCTE is provided mostly at the cost of the participating organisation and the individual's personal time.

The components that need to converge, or at least co-exist in a planned way, are already well known and include those listed in Figure 5.11:

• Meta-meta models	• Object naming and identity schemes
• Meta models	• Version control mechanisms
• Import/export language	• Configuration management
• Services interfaces	• Partitioning strategies

Figure 5.11 Areas for standards harmonisation

For all three standards more work is needed in the area of conformance. This includes the definition of conformance levels and the means by which conformance to these levels is certified. The CASE users' expectation is that if one tool conforms to Standard X at Level A and another tool conforms to Standard X at Level A then they should be able to interchange data. It is appreciated, however, that this is not a simple area and that there are a number of factors and levels involved in any conforming tool.

The issue of information dissemination also needs to be addressed. As someone who has had to work through a large number of standards-related documents in the course of producing this paper, the author feels the information was much less accessible and understandable than it could have been!

The current IRDS and PCTE documentation is either too abstract or too detailed (written for example largely in SQL and PASCAL in the case of IRDS) to enable it to be understood quickly by the reader. It also refers to terms in too many other documents not available to the average reader. Some thought should be given to construction of some more easily digested, self-contained documentation containing examples to supplement the standard documentation set. (The CDIF documentation set is an excellent example in this respect).

CDIF need to give careful consideration regarding the future evolution and management of their meta modelling work. Mechanisms and resourcing must be put in place for the following:

- request for subject area inputs (cf. OMG Request for Technology);
- evaluation and consensus gaining on new subject areas;
- management of changes to existing subject areas (e.g. OOA enhancements to ER);
- strategy regarding one superset or many different meta models;
- management, release and notification of new meta model versions.

Failure to address these issues could result in their meta model not developing quickly enough to meet CASE users' needs and the pendulum perhaps swinging back in favour of the less open approaches!

7.5 A final word

CASE data integration around open/international standards is not here yet but it really seems to be on its way over the next three to five years.

CDIF would seem to offer a good start-point through addressing the immediate and prerequisite problem of data interchange.

If liaison between the CDIF, PCTE and IRDS groups continues to take place in a good spirit then there is a strong chance that a mix and match consolidation of their work will form the basis for open data integration around a repository.

There are, however, still a number of difficult questions, not least of which is whether, in the long term, we need (or can afford) both PCTE and IRDS?

6 Providing Generic CASE Integration

Andrew Mercer
Software One Limited

1 INTRODUCTION

This paper covers some of the current problems in systems development and, more specifically, the issues arising from attempts to automate development using CASE. An increasing number of organisations, both CASE users and major tool vendors, see integration as being critical to the successful adoption of CASE by the development community.

The remainder of this document comprises four sections:

1 **Why CASE is unavoidable**

IT management faces a number of challenges which are now forcing many companies to adopt a rigorous CASE-based approach to developing systems.

2 **Experiences with CASE**

Many organisations using CASE tools and methods have encountered significant problems which have inhibited effective implementation. This section examines the barriers to success which they (and the CASE industry) have identified, and the implications of failure.

3 **The solution framework**

How organisations are starting to break down these barriers by identifying missing components in their CASE strategies, such as the provision of automatic tool interfacing. Furthermore, the measures necessary to achieve effective CASE integration can help organisations to prepare for a repository (whether from IBM or another supplier).

2 WHY CASE IS UNAVOIDABLE

The goal of IS managers is to improve the quality of the service they provide to their users, in an environment where the needs of businesses and the information technology available are changing more quickly than IS departments are able to assimilate. In trying to attain this goal, the IS function faces a number of pressures:

- Developers are endeavouring to remain flexible in their response to changing demands yet improve the speed of their delivery. At the same time, advances in technology have allowed increasingly sophisticated applications to be built. These are necessarily more complicated than ever before, so developers are always grappling with new uncertainties. IS organisations are finding that this very fluid situation, with change requests extending right through the life cycle, means that applications are effectively in maintenance before they are even delivered. No wonder maintenance costs are always greater than those of the original development effort.
- Increasingly, the value of an organization's data is being recognized. By treating data as a corporate asset and co-ordinating the use of that data in different but related applications, organizations have been able to achieve more flexibility and greater benefits from their systems.
- IS has always been focused on helping end-users to access the information they need in order to perform various business functions. Now, for the first time, the IT industry is realising that most of the information it needs for its own functions is locked away in the physical database definitions and the code for existing systems. What is more, there is a huge amount of it.
- Senior management is in many cases disillusioned with the performance of their IS function and are expecting to see changes in approach to give the desired improvement.

In other areas of industry, the goals of increased productivity, consistent quality, and reduced cost have been achieved only through increasing automation; examples which come to mind are manufacturing processes and financial/accounting systems. The visionaries in IT recognised the parallel some years ago. In order to enable the systems development function to satisfy the increasing demands of its users, automating systems development is the only solution; hence CASE was developed amid great expectations that it would solve all these problems. CASE is really application software for IS professionals.

3 EXPERIENCE WITH CASE

Unfortunately, the great expectations of CASE remain as yet largely unfulfilled. The evidence to support this is pretty conclusive. A Price Waterhouse report showed that about a third of all organisations have experience of CASE, but closer investigation reveals that only about one in ten of their developers are actually using the CASE tools that have been bought. At less than 4 per cent the market penetration and actual use of CASE begins to look rather poor. No wonder the senior vice-president at Softlab, Helmut Coqui, recently remarked that Companies spend more on coffee for systems developers than they do on CASE tools!

Perhaps the most significant indicator of the unfulfilled expectations of CASE is that IT management are often only luke-warm supporters. Project managers should be the most ardent believers in the possibilities of CASE, since they have the most to gain by getting things done better and quicker; but when push comes to shove, very few believe that CASE can help them deliver systems quicker. They abandon CASE tools and revert to the good old ways (see Figure 6.1).

Figure 6.1 The good old ways...

Contrast this with the attitude of application software companies. Many package suppliers are now using CASE to develop their software.

If we look at the current integration strategies of most organisations using CASE, the tool users tend to communicate the results of their work to each other on pieces of paper, using data models, action diagrams, DDL scripts, etc. The analyst, the designer (and even the user) discuss, argue and negotiate the development process, based on these pieces of paper.

There are a number of barriers to improving this situation, including:

- people's natural aversion to change, and their preference for old familiar ways;

- the lack of a standard method, understood and used by developers;
- a generally low level of understanding of the role and capability of CASE, a lack of commitment and investment, and a lack of education in individual tool use.

But the consistent message coming from industry experts, such as Russell Jones, and CASE users like our customers, is that one of the most significant barriers is the lack of adequate integration. And what we mean by effective CASE integration is not just the transfer of information from one CASE tool to another down the life cycle, rather it is the integration of various CASE components around a common dictionary/repository.

For whether you believe that the ultimate solution is to buy everything from one vendor (integrated CASE or I-CASE), each tool from a different vendor (component CASE or C-CASE), or even a combination of I-CASE tools from different vendors, no solution will work really effectively without a repository at its heart. Although a full repository does not exist now, we believe that organisations need to prepare for it, and the more far-sighted ones are already doing this by sharing information via a data dictionary or encyclopedia.

The limiting factor in getting benefits from a repository will not be the technology: rather it will be the rate at which organisations can change their working practices to accommodate the technology.

So in summary:

- CASE is unavoidable: it is the only viable means of automating the applications manufacturing process;
- but we know CASE is only half working (at best!); and
- the major barrier to success is the lack of integration around a common dictionary/repository.

The implication for IS management of not facing up to the challenge of making CASE work in their organisation is that they will not achieve the goals that they have been set by the users, i.e. improved quality and productivity, and better value for money.

4 THE SOLUTION FRAMEWORK

The only solution to the problem of unlocking the potential of CASE is to create a framework within which it is possible to:

- Migrate information
  Take information about your application systems that has been captured in CASE tools and migrate it through the different stages in the development life cycle, paying particular attention to information which is required later in the life cycle, or which may be reusable in subsequent projects.

- Prepare for repository
  Begin to prepare for the availability of a repository by defining the role that it can play, now and in the future, in the development environment.
- Protect investment
  Implement new CASE tools (and replace existing ones) without any loss of investment in the information about systems that is already captured in current tools. This is obviously a prime consideration; it also confers a measure of independence from any individual tool vendor! It is worth remembering that strategic tool purchase is really a myth: very few tools are implemented for more than three years with no changes.

For development support people, implementing this solution is a prime mission statement for the next few years.

To date, most people using CASE tools have focused on the first requirement, migrating information by linking various tools. This is usually still done manually, but some development shops use an automated one-way bridge between two tools, for example between an analysis tool like IEW, and a code generator such as TELON. The IT department may also have spent considerable time defining their corporate meta model in a dictionary (although few data administrators would agree that this is used properly).

So IT professionals quite often know what they are trying to achieve, and many are aware of the benefits that CASE can bring. But we have discovered that in fact very few have a firm idea of exactly how to put their plans into action. In fact, there is no chance of overall success unless the framework is established, then all three aspects of the solution can be tackled concurrently.

We shall deal with the preparation for repository later. First, a look at how a generic CASE tool interface provides the other two elements of the framework. Software One EXCHANGE enables customers to integrate all current and future CASE components according to a consistent standard and to assert their data dictionary as the heart of the development infrastructure.

4.1 Exchange

Conceptually, the software is like a plug bar providing an interface between CASE tools supporting different stages in the life cycle. This represents one element of the solution framework: automating the migration of data.

The data dictionary or repository drives and controls the whole operation, and EXCHANGE provides the facility to plug in and unplug tools at every phase of development. This then represents another aspect of the framework: customers are free to buy new tools and replace old ones with no loss in their investment in the information already captured, and no expensive re-keying. Thus options are kept open with regard to future changes.

So how does it work? The tool can be considered as a black box with gateways to disparate CASE components. Information comes in at one end from various upper CASE tools and dictionaries, and out the other to upper CASE tools, dictionaries, and lower CASE tools.

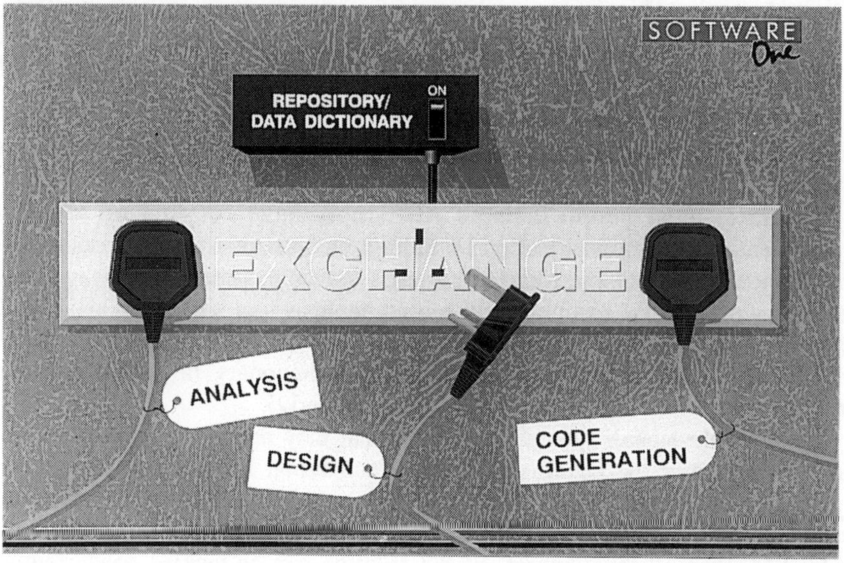

Figure 6.2 The EXCHANGE plug bar

Because these tools support different stages in the life cycle, they have different structures (or meta models) for representing information. The interface can accommodate all the different tools and their meta models, and move information from the conceptual level of analysis to the logical level; and then, if required, to the physical level required for code generation.

This flexibility is achieved by using a specific rule set for each supported tool to decode data into a generic format, independent of the source. The information is then manipulated in the internal information resource dictionary (IRD) as necessary. When the information has reached the level required, more rule sets are invoked to perform encode processing specific to the chosen target.

The EXCHANGE architecture is divided into three distinct modules: for the transference processes (decode and encode); for the inference processes; and for our transient IRD and the user interface. We shall look at each of these in turn, beginning with the heart of EXCHANGE: the internal database where the incoming data is accommodated after being decoded into a generic format.

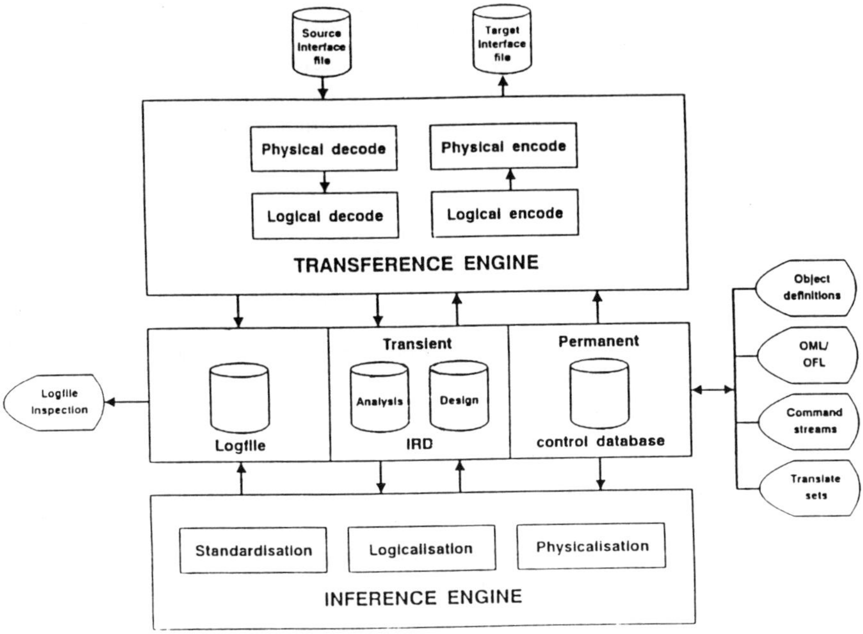

Figure 6.3 EXCHANGE architecture

4.1.1 The IRD

This data repository is essentially transient: it contains only one version at a time, and cannot be inspected. It is split into two areas, supporting separate meta models for analysis and design. Broadly, the distinction between these is that analysis objects represent the definition of a requirement, and design objects are used in the implementation of the requirement. For example, an entity is an analysis object, and a table is a design object.

4.1.2 The inference engine

When migrating data between tools, EXCHANGE moves from one meta model to another and across levels. It uses what we call the inference processes:

- Standardisation
  This is used to enable EXCHANGE to recognise the data: it converts incoming data types to EXCHANGE data types, generates missing domains, and orders relationships. It also incorporates basic integrity checking: for

example, ensuring that an entity record does not refer to a non-existent attribute.

- Logicalisation
  This moves data from the conceptual analysis level to the logical analysis level. Specific operations involved are: generating identifiers for entities (where missing in the input); and resolving exclusive relationship sets, super-/sub-entity groups, many-to-many relationships.
- Physicalisation
  Here the information is moved from a logical analysis model to the physical design level. EXCHANGE infers tables and fields from entities and attributes and resolves identifiers and relationships into foreign keys and indexes.
  We have found that some sites physicalise their entity model in the upper CASE tool. To avoid generating duplicate fields, physicalisation can be switched off where necessary.

Validation ensures the completeness and logical consistency of the input. There are fixed message points, and modifiable severity levels for posting messages to the logfile. These are customisable, and users can define their own error messages.

EXCHANGE therefore provides an effective check that certain site standards are observed (and even that the source tool is being used properly). When we started, we thought we were simply transferring data. However, one customer is also using EXCHANGE to enforce naming conventions: synonyms used by different projects are converted into a single name as part of the transfer to the dictionary, so enquiry and impact analysis are improved. Another customer uses EXCHANGE to support quality assurance.

4.1.3 The transference engine

When transferring data into and out of EXCHANGE, the physical and logical aspects of decode and encode have been separated to give more precise control. We have written the Object Formatting Language (OFL) and the Object Mapping Language (OML) to perform the physical decode/encode and logical decode/ encode respectively. Together, these represent a flexible meta tool for building interfaces; in fact, we are licensing several customers and vendors to use OML and OFL to develop their own interfaces to EXCHANGE.

4.1.4 The control model

The permanent control database accommodates the OML/OFL rule sets, selection of the SLP processes, etc. In readiness for providing multi-platform support, the User Interface is XVT, a library kit for building screens independent of the GUI.

4.1.5 Supported tools

EXCHANGE currently moves information from tools supporting the conceptual phase to tools supporting the logical phase and, if required, to tools supporting the physical design phase of the life cycle. The specific tools currently supported or under development are shown in Figure 6.4. Those shown in brackets are planned.

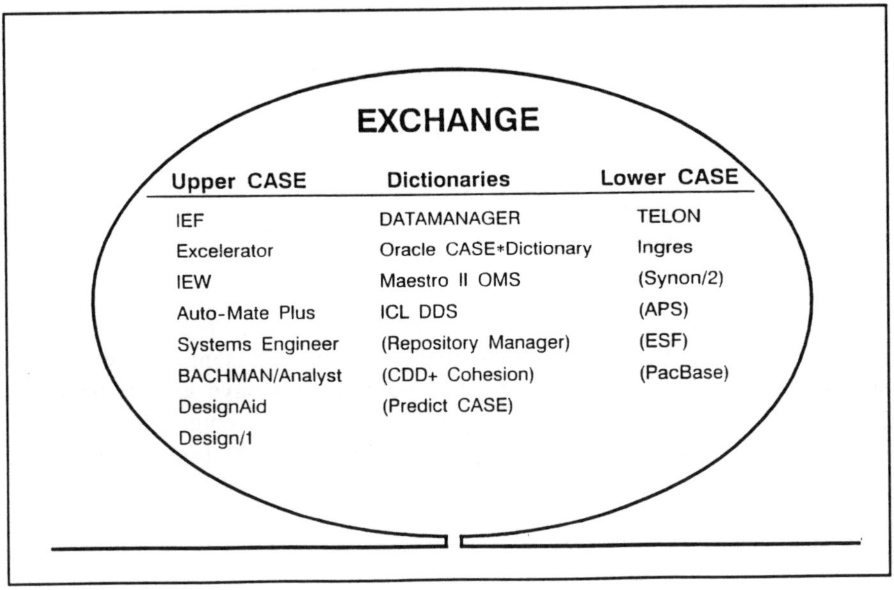

Figure 6.4 EXCHANGE interfaces

Interestingly, information can already be exchanged between tools at the same level, whether supporting the conceptual or logical stages in the life cycle; for instance, between IEF and IEW, or between DATAMANAGER and DDS. Future versions of the product will have the ability to exchange information between different tools supporting the physical design phase as well.

4.2 Preparing for repository

No interfacing tool can operate in a vacuum. It is clear that, as in any manufacturing operation, CASE sites must be geared up: in order to cope with automation, a culture involving a certain amount of discipline is essential. This is an outline of the appropriate action to be taken at different levels of an organization.

There are certain key elements of any plan for the creation of the framework for viable CASE integration. Some of the technical requirements are:

- define meta model objects;
- define links with methodology, tools and techniques;
- define mapping rules;
- implement automated interfacing.

And before we even get to that stage there are high level business issues which must be resolved. Like any other type of corporate planning, this requires the allocation of responsibility and authority to individuals involved. Such considerations include:

- organisational structures;
- master versus slave;
- collision management.

In addition to constituting the basis of an effective future repository strategy, resolution of all these issues (and many others) is essential **now** for the productive use of any CASE tool set. IT departments have to face up to the possible cultural changes whether or not automatic interfacing is implemented.

Proper use of tools within an integrated environment brings results, and this in turn empowers those in development support to enforce the use of the tools. Software One has gained unique experience in these areas by helping customers with the challenges they have faced.

5 SUMMARY

CASE has so far not been meeting the expectations of users and management. It is becoming increasingly clear, however, that this is not only a failing of CASE technology itself, but also of education in CASE use.

There are two dimensions to the CASE integration issue:

- strategic: assimilation of tools and practices into organisations and procedures;
- tactical: automatic interfacing between individual tools.

A shortfall in both the above areas has led to the inadequate and often inappropriate use of CASE tools, which in turn has diminished the perceived value of CASE. So the present lack of integration constitutes the critical barrier to progress in systems development.

Anyone preparing for repository and trying to migrate information between different tools and dictionaries will already know that overcoming the integration barrier is no trivial task. IT departments can, however, realise the potential of CASE by instituting the framework described in this paper.

Many large corporations have already implemented an effective integration strategy and are now beginning to achieve significant tangible benefits from their chosen CASE tools.

REFERENCES

Price Waterhouse (1990) *IT Review 1989/1990*, Price Waterhouse, London.

Part Three

CASE Frameworks and User Experiences

7 The Atherton Software BackPlane

Eric Black
Principal Architect, Atherton Technology, USA

1 INTRODUCTION

A variety of productivity enhancements tools are in use today to address the problems encountered in large, complex software projects, including Computer Aided Software Engineering (CASE) tools to assist the software design process, project planning and resource management tools, documentation and traceability tools, and more traditional programming support tools such as symbolic debuggers and database management systems. A typical project environment is made up of a suite of these tools that address the various phases of the systems development life cycle, or perhaps span several or all phases. The problem is that unless these tools can work together to share data and resources, and unless that sharing and the development process itself are explicitly represented by, and manipulable as, data, their influence on the project's overall success is severely limited.

Integration of the various development tools into a cohesive environment can yield a logical view of a single tool with many capabilities. For example, rather than having a document layout tool and a configuration management tool and a project management tool, the user (and his manager) have an environment tool which has document formatting, configuration management, and project tracking functions. An Integrated Project Support Environment (IPSE) provides the infrastructure for project management including data sharing, configuration management, work-flow control, data distribution, and portability of tools, data, and users.

Software BackPlane is an IPSE which meets these requirements. Users can easily extend and customise the environment by creating new classes and new methods, integrating the tools of their choice and not merely the tools chosen by the environment vendor. Potentially complex customisations are simplified by the object-oriented programming metaphor, which includes an object-class hierarchy with inheritance of both attributes and behaviour, and object persistence in a distributed database.

This paper describes some of the Software BackPlane features which facilitate integration of tools with the environment and with other tools, and explains the support for automating and enforcing the development process and work flow as defined by the customer. A brief summary of ATIS (A Tool Integration Standard) is presented, and its relationship to PCTE (Portable Common Tool Environment) is discussed. Finally, an overview of future directions for Software BackPlane with regard to ATIS, PCTE, and emerging technologies such as BMS (Broadcast Message Service) and ToolTalk is given.

2 ARCHITECTURE OF SOFTWARE BACKPLANE

First, it is appropriate to present a brief overview of the object-oriented concepts and terms used in Software BackPlane and in this paper. Note that the use of an object-oriented programming language, such as Smalltalk, C++, Objective-C, Eiffel, and so on, is not required in order to use an object-oriented model. In fact, for an IPSE, with which tools and applications written in perhaps many different languages must be integrated, it is important that a particular programming language not be required, and that bindings for a variety of languages can be created. In the case of Software BackPlane, the programming language used is standard portable C. This choice carries with it the implication that some types of compile-time checking and optimisations cannot be applied, but many can be performed either at run time (with some penalty in performance), or by a separate checker (in much the same way that lint performs more compile-time error checking than do most C compilers), or a combination of the two.

An object is a separately identified unit of data, and each object is an instance of a class (called a type in Software BackPlane). Each object class is defined in terms of:

- the messages to which an instance responds (i.e., the public function interface specifications);
- the methods which implement those messages (i.e., function bodies);
- the instance variables (persistent attributes, normally visible only to the method functions).

Thus, an object embodies not only the data but also (via its class) the interfaces to, and the semantics of, the allowable operations on that data.

Objects are manipulated only through the public interface, that is, only by sending messages. As is typical in object-oriented polymorphism, the message sent and the class of the object to which it is sent determine the method function invoked.

Classes are hierarchically ordered, with single inheritance of messages, methods, and attributes. The object-oriented inheritance features of the Software BackPlane class hierarchy help to minimise the code required to integrate a tool or application. Each class defined by the tool integrator inherits the interfaces, the attributes, and the behaviours of its superclass. By refining that inherited definition, the tool integrator fleshes out the new class definition and provides only that part of the new definition which differs from what is inherited from the superclass.

Refinement by adding new attributes is straightforward; the new class has those new attributes in addition to those inherited from the superclass. Refinement by adding new messages is similarly straightforward; every message the superclass has, the new class also has, plus whatever additional new messages the class implementor defines. The definitions of messages and attributes inherited from the superclass cannot be changed. However, the behaviour of an inherited message can be changed as needed, as long as it matches the interface definition (i.e. the message arguments and returned values) defined for the message. The inherited behaviour can even by refined to return a special error such as ILLEGAL_OPERATION, thereby making the inherited message inoperable.

In general, the behaviour of a class differs from its superclass by adding specialisation. Usually there is something new that is done first, followed by whatever would be done by the superclass, or something new that is done after doing whatever is done by the superclass, or both. In rare cases, the inherited behaviour is completely replaced by new behaviour. The invocation of the behaviour inherited from the superclass is done quite simply from within the refined method function using the special message dispatch function dispatchSuper(), which automatically determines the superclass and invokes the correct method function.

Thus a typical method function consists of three parts, any of which may be absent or empty:

- do something first (the preamble);
- do whatever is inherited from the superclass (by calling dispatchSuper()) or do something new (the method body);
- do something afterwards (the postamble).

The preamble and postamble are themselves methods. This means that they also have a method body, and can have a preamble and /or postamble. Each method function is represented by a METHOD object in the repository; that object either contains the method function code itself (in any supported programming or script language) or has stored attributes which identify and represent a method function whose code is provided elsewhere (such as in an executable programme). Preamble and postamble methods can be added to an existing method by adding them to preamble and postamble attributes on the METHOD object. Thus, refinements to an inherited method can be stacked merely by manipulating objects in the database, and source code for the inherited method is not required. This is extremely useful both for integrating new tools and for enforcing work-flow control rules.

The advantage of this approach is that a tool integrator or environment customiser can automatically gain the benefits provided by the built-in classes of Software BackPlane with little or no effort. In general, the tool integrator defines a class for every distinct kind of object which is to be represented in the project repository. For coarse-grained (file level) data, these classes can correspond to the different file classes and filename extensions of tool data when stored in the native file system, for example the class C_SOURCE corresponds to files with filename extensions of .c and C_INCLUDE to files with extensions of .h. The only work to be done is in characterising the tool (a non-trivial task, to be sure) and augmenting the behaviour and attributes inherited from the built-in classes based on judicious choice of location in the class hierarchy for the new class or classes. Because of the object-oriented inheritance of Software BackPlane, the user of a tool can then obtain the version management, configuration management, and work-flow control features of Software BackPlane without the tool even being aware of them. Of course, a tool which is aware of Software BackPlane and of other tools which are integrated gains even greater benefit.

3 WHY IS SOFTWARE BACKPLANE OBJECT-ORIENTED?

Release 1.0 of Software BackPlane (in 1987) was based on an Entity-Relationship (ER) model. The work reflected in IRDS, PCTE 1.4, and CAIS-A was carefully considered in the design of the base-level environment. As we extended the environment by adding more tools and more types of tool data, we found the number of public functions literally exploding. Yet at the same time, classification of those types into a hierarchical ordering was quite natural. The problem was that, as is the case in PCTE, while the attributes were inherited along the type hierarchy, the behaviours were not, resulting in an explosive growth in the number of procedural interfaces with each incremental extension to the environment. Enforcement of integrity constraints, especially mutual constraints between two different pieces of data, could not be guaranteed because the type implementor was forced to be aware of the constraints (or at least the name of the entry point for the constraint checker) and to explicitly perform the check. Adding an object-oriented type manager and message dispatch mechanism allowed us to reduce the more than 450 ER procedural interfaces to 17 object-oriented message interfaces, and removed the requirement for every type implementor to have knowledge of implementational details of other types in the type hierarchy.

The type manager also allowed us to add the concept of triggers. A trigger is a piece of code which must be executed either before or after a method.

Parameters passed to the trigger are the same as those passed to the method. This allows enforcement of go/no-go decisions on a per-operation basis, and allows for easy extension of the existing system by stacking set-up and clean-up triggers before and after an existing method, and provides a mechanism on which notifications can conveniently be implemented.

Security on a per-object basis is added at the level of the type manager, allowing for finer resolution of access permissions than the typical Read, Write, Delete granularity found in non-message-based systems. Because every operation on an object is performed by sending a message to the object, access permissions on the message object or on the method object which represents the method function provides much more flexible control than that accorded by placing all access checks on the object being manipulated.

In summary, object orientation allows Software BackPlane to meet the requirements of ease of extensibility, administrative control, integrity enforcement, data integration, control integration, customisability, reusability, security and evolution much more readily.

4 OVERVIEW OF ATIS

ATIS (A Tool Integration Standard) is intended to address issues of control and data integration which must be solved for all tool integrations. Unless standard solutions to these issues are agreed upon, each tool integrator must solve them independently, and the effectiveness of the resulting environment can be expected to suffer. ATIS was originated in 1988 by Atherton Technology and Digital Equipment Corporation, but its continuing evolution has been carried on by the CASE Integration Services (CIS) Committee, an industry consortium of environment providers, hardware vendors, CASE tool vendors, and end users.

ATIS defines a number of semantic models. Some of these models are identified but at present unspecified in ATIS. That is, their importance is recognised, and their place is identified in the ATIS documents, but they are not yet defined.

The semantic models defined by ATIS are:

- Basic object-oriented data model; objects, messages, methods
  A minimal type (class) hierarchy with at least single inheritance of both attributes and behaviour. This model does not require an object-oriented internal architecture; the interface to the services specified in this model follows the object-oriented model of behavioural polymorphism accessed by sending messages to objects. The minimal type hierarchy includes only those types required to implement the basic object-oriented data model. It requires the services of an underlying persistent repository, but does not specify the interface to that repository. ATIS can just as readily be implemented using,

for example, an object-oriented database, an entity-relationship database, or a relational database.

- Versioning model
  Introduces new types and new messages to support a model of object mutability combined with the ability to take snapshots of an object; the snapshots are linked together with predecessor/successor relationships which indicate the genealogy of the data. New versions are created as mutable copies of their predecessor (as a result of sending the reserve message to the predecessor), and can be changed until such time as they are made immutable (by sending them the replace message).
- Configuration model (composite objects)
  Provides a model for grouping specific versions of objects into a configuration which can then be manipulated as a single entity, and is itself versioned.
- Work-flow control model
  Adds types and semantics which can be used to enforce project development methods and policies, but does not define a specific work flow or design method.
- Tool integration/client registration model
  Provides the mechanism for extending the environment by adding new tools and applications, including defining new types, new messages, new implementations of messages (i.e. method functions). Features are added to simplify data and control integration of an existing tool and requiring no, or minimal, modification of the tool (non-intrusive).
- Transaction model
  Introduces the notion of atomicity of operations. A nested transaction model is specified, but the precise semantics of the model are as yet unspecified (still To Be Done).
- Security model
  Currently provides only for discretionary access control; mandatory access control is possible but not required by ATIS. Defines basic access rights (Read, Write, Execute, Delete, etc.), and applies them to the object-oriented model. Because the access permissions can be applied to message and method objects as well as project data, very fine control over operations and not just data objects can be obtained. Reconciliation of the ATIS security model with that of PCTE is a desirable goal, and one which is not thought to be particularly difficult; until that is accomplished, however, the security model of ATIS is To Be Done.
- Name services model
  Provides for mapping in both directions between an object's internal name (its unique object ID) and a human-readable external name. This is still To Be Done.

- Correspondence model
  Provides facilities to meet the requirements of traceability. Some relationships between components need to be updated automatically whenever the components participating in the relationships are updated; others must not be updated, but should result in the notification of the owner(s) of the components that the other component in the relationship has changed. This implies that relationships must be first-class objects in the ATIS data model so as to allow for type-specific refinement of the behaviour of the relationships. Unfortunately, this tends to conflict with the requirement that they be sufficiently light-weight that very large numbers of relationships may be stored and manipulated efficiently. Pending resolution of the conflict, this portion of the ATIS specification is To Be Done.

5 RELATIONSHIP OF ATIS TO PCTE

First, it must be understood that ATIS and PCTE are in no way competitive or interchangeable specifications. On the contrary, they are for the most part complementary, and both are desirable in a software development environment. Recall that the acronym PCTE originally stood for A **Basis** for a Portable Common Tool Environment [emphasis added]. PCTE is not an environment, nor is it a specification for an environment; it is a specification for a framework, a set of building blocks from which an environment can be built. Nor is ATIS an environment; ATIS specifies services and interfaces to those services to enhance tool integration and customisation of the tools within an environment. Neither PCTE nor ATIS specifies a complete environment, but together they specify many of the services which are used by the environment builder, the tool implementor or integrator, and the environment customiser.

ATIS specifically addresses tool integration services. It assumes that conforming environments will have solved the portability problem separately. One such solution is to use the portability services provided by PCTE. Thus, ATIS should be complementary to PCTE, and should be able to use PCTE as a portable base on which to provide integration services.

The following taxonomy might be drawn illustrating the different connotations of the terms platform, framework, IPSE, and SDE. As the figure suggests, PCTE is an example of a specification for a framework, building on the platform-level services provided by the POSIX and X specifications to provide the low-level infrastructure and capabilities (such as portability, a repository, inter-process communication, transactions, etc.) which are needed to construct an IPSE. Another example of framework-level services is represented by Motif, indicating the presentation and user interface services which are used by an IPSE to provide seamless look and feel. A Broadcast Message Service such as that used in HP's SoftBench, Sun's ToolTalk, and other products is shown as a framework-level service; the BMS box is dashed because at present there is no standard or specification for BMS messages.

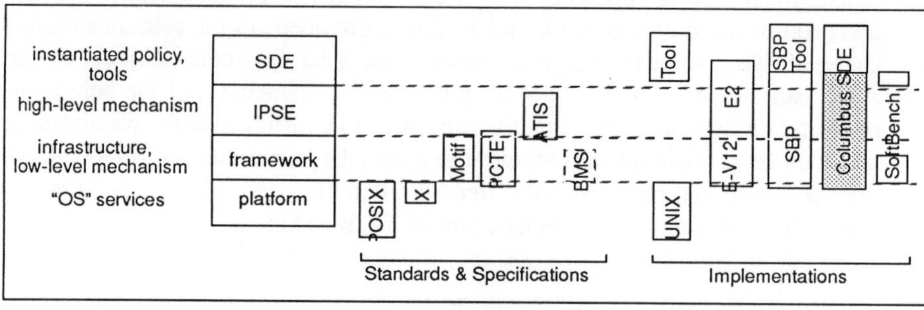

ATIS is an example of one of the several aspects of an IPSE which builds on the features provided by the underlying framework to provide a higher-level abstraction of the mechanisms which form the general-purpose IPSE. An SDE is the fully integrated project support environment, populated by the tools which are integrated with the environment and with each other to form the integrated toolset used by the project. The SDE includes the customisations of the IPSE to implement policy using the mechanisms provided by the IPSE with the underlying framework. Implementations (products) based on the respective standards are represented by UNIX, Emeraude V12, Entreprise2, Software BackPlane, and the Columbus SDE (which is based on Software BackPlane). As indicated in the diagram, products almost necessarily span a wider range than a standard or standards.

Qualitatively, ATIS is object-oriented with entity relationships added as a straightforward extension to the model, whereas PCTE is entity-relationship based with some object orientation added, specifically, inheritance of attributes but no encapsulation and inheritance of behaviour (code).

Both PCTE and ATIS have the notion of attributed objects with individual identity, but PCTE emphasises identification of objects by navigating to them, and ATIS makes the object identity and its use explicit. Both have relationships (links) between objects. Both have the idea of different versions of the same data by using successor-predecessor relationships between objects representing those versions. Both have composition of objects into configurations.

ATIS provides encapsulation of behaviour in the form of methods which are associated with the type and not with the tool. This encapsulation allows integrity constraints to be enforced because all manipulation of the state (attributes) of an object is done exclusively through those method functions, invoked via the public message interface; attributes (including relationships) are never manipulated directly by a tool or application, so constraints enforced by the method code are always enforced and cannot be bypassed. It also facilitates sharing of functionality because a particular function or operation may be used by many without requiring each one to provide the code which performs that function.

PCTE specifies multiple inheritance (of attributes), but ATIS requires only single inheritance, and allows a conforming implementation to have multiple inheritance.

Another difference is that objects in PCTE tend to be fairly heavyweight; the overhead of a minimal object is of the order of 128 bytes. Tools tend to store data in objects which correspond roughly to files, with finer-grained data stored inside those objects in private formats. ATIS encourages finer-grained storage of tool data in objects much smaller than files so that other tools have visibility of that data without resorting to private interfaces between the tools. For performance reasons, a tool may still store data in a private format within a coarse-grained object, but may publish portions of that data for other tools by copying the actual internally-used data to fine-grained objects whose format and meaning are published in the repository schema.

6 FUTURE DIRECTIONS FOR SOFTWARE BACKPLANE

The current market confusion over software development environments is unfortunate. The four major technologies contributing to this confusion seem to be:

- PCTE (represented by products such as Emeraude V12);
- ATIS (represented by products such as Software BackPlane);
- message-based architectures (represented by products such as SoftBench and ToolTalk);
- file-based architectures (represented by products such as NSE, built using advanced features of NFS technology).

As has been shown, PCTE and ATIS are complementary, rather than competing, approaches to a complete solution. Similarly, the technologies represented by BMS and NFS are not alternative solutions but instead bring additional, complementary features and capabilities towards a full solution.

The Broadcast Message Service (BMS) as used by SoftBench from Hewlett Packard, ToolTalk from Sun Microsystems, Fuse from Digital Equipment Corporation, and other products based on the technology developed at Brown University in the FIELD project, provides improved responsiveness and usability of tools used by the individual developer, so-called Programming In The Small (PITS) tools. The tight edit-compile-debug cycle of the code developer and the edit-preview-print cycle of the documenter are examples of PITS situations. Such users often are slowed down by the imposition of Programming In The Large (PITL) tools and work flow rules, resulting in enthusiastic bypassing of those rules. The BMS approach helps the tool integrator and the environment customiser to maximise habit preservation on the part of the individual developer when process changes such as stricter rules are imposed as the project progresses in its development, and allows timely response which can help alleviate the desire to bypass the environment.

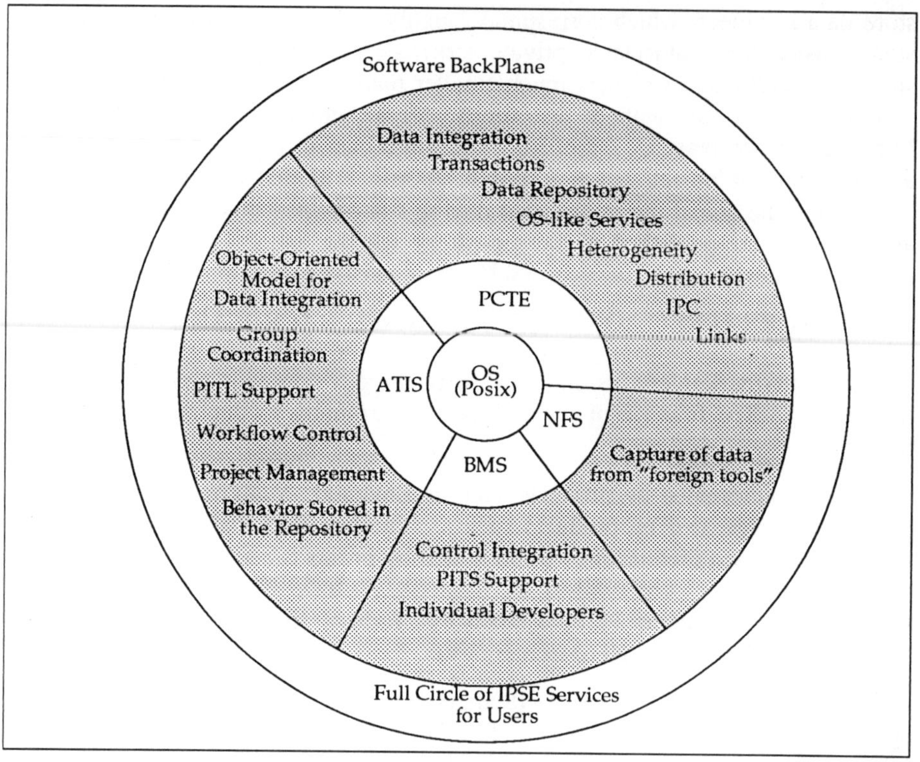

Generalising the message-passing metaphor to include not only broadcast or multicast inter-process messages as is provided by BMS, but also directed messages to fine-grained objects, is a natural and expected result of combining

ATIS and BMS technologies with the work being done by the Object Management Group (OMG) on the Object Request Broker (ORB) specification.

The file-based approach (intercepting apparently ordinary file system references and routing them to the environment repository) as used in NSE from Sun Microsystems is helpful in dealing with the migration from existing tools which are unaware of the environment to tools which are engineered to participate fully in the environment. Tool data granularity is constrained to be that of files, but the data can be stored in the environment repository, can be described in the meta-data (schema) in the environment repository, and can be share by other tools which are integrated with the environment or which are simply referring to the same files.

As the figure shows, the features and services of a complete IPSE, shown in the shaded outer circle, are provided by the various contributors which are not competing but are working together to provide what is needed to help solve the problems of the individual developer in the PITS as well as the PITL problems of the manager.

7 SUMMARY

Software BackPlane includes a number of features designed to facilitate the integration of existing tools as well as the creation of new tools which are engineered to make use of the services provided by an IPSE. These features may be exploited to help automate and enforce the development process and work-flow as defined by the customer. The object-oriented model and interface of Software BackPlane makes such customisation possible to a much greater extent than in traditional environment architectures.

A number of standards and technologies, including ATIS, PCTE, BMS, NFS, and others, may be used in combination to yield a powerful environment which provides a full circle of necessary services to the user of an IPSE. The continuing evolution of Software BackPlane will take advantage of these and other standards as they emerge.

REFERENCES

Black, E. (1989) Software Configuration Management with an Object-Oriented Database, Proceedings of the 1989 Winter USENIX Technical Conference, San Diego.

Black, E. (1991a) Tool Integration Approaches in an Object-Oriented IPSE, Proceedings of the 5th International TOOLS USA. Conference, Santa Barbara (July-August 1991), Prentice Hall.

Black, E. (1991b) ATIS, CIS, PCTE, and Software BackPlane, to appear in Proceedings of the 4th Toulouse International Conference on Software Engineering and its Applications, Toulouse.

Cagan, M. (1990) The HP SoftBench Environment: An Architecture for a New Generation of Software Tools, *Hewlett-Packard Journal*, June 1990.

CASE Integration Services (CIS) Committee (1991) CIS Base Document V1.0.

Courington, W., Feiber, J., and Honda, M. (1988) NSE Highlights, *Sun Technology: The Journal for Sun Users*, Winter 1988.

Department of Defense (1988) Defense System Software Development, Military Standard DOD-STD-2167A, February 1988.

European Computer Manufacturers' Association (1990) ECMA PCTE Standard, ECMA-149, December 1990.

Electronic Industry Association (1991) CDIF: Framework for Modeling and Extensibility, EIA-PN2387.

Independent European Programme Group Technical Area 13 (1989) Introducing PCTE+.

Matthews, E. and Burns, G. (1990) VADS APSE: An Integrated Ada Programming Support Environment, Proceedings of the First Symposium on Environments and Tools for Ada, Redondo Beach.

Nolan, C. (1988) CATIS Requirements and Goals, available from CIS secretary.

Paseman, W. (1988) Architecture of an Integration and Portability Platform, Digest of Papers from the Spring 1988 CompCon Conference, San Francisco.

Paseman, W. (1989) Tools on a New Level, *UNIX Review*, 7(6).

Reiss, S. (1987) Overview of the FIELD Environment, Brown University, Department of Computer Science.

van Riel, W. (1991) Integrated Project Support Environments: Benefits and Functions, Proceedings of the International Workshop on UNIX-Based Software Development Environments, Dallas.

8 The Columbus SDE – An Overview

Henrik Maegaard and Jesper Andersen
Computer Resources International A/S, Denmark[1]

This paper gives an overview of the Columbus Software Development Environment (CSDE). CSDE is built for use in software development within the Columbus manned space program sponsored by the European Space Agency (ESA).

CSDE is offered to the Columbus consortium as the main cornerstone in the software process. It supports a classic waterfall model as defined by ESA standard PSS-05. The main emphasis is placed on utilization of Commercial-Off-The-Shelf (COTS) tools integrated in an objected-oriented environment facilitating a 'plug-in/ plug-out' paradigm.

The present paper will address details on the kind of large-scale projects that will be supported, the design and integration platform chosen, implementation of the integration strategy, as well as the importance of an object-oriented approach. Furthermore, the importance of procurement, deployment, and support strategy will be discussed.

1 THE COLUMBUS PROGRAM

The ambitious European goal of establishing a permanently manned, autonomous space station in orbit in the beginning of the next century is meant to be initiated by the Columbus program.

In its current shape, the Columbus manned space program is tied closely to the success of the International Space Station Freedom.

Its two main elements are the Attached Pressurized Module (APM) and the Man-Tended Free Flyer (MTFF). A Polar Platform (un-manned) is planned for orbit by the end of the century and is conducted as a separate project, but it will utilize Columbus software development technology.

---

1 CRI is the main contractor on the COLUMBUS SDE.

The development of CSDE is being funded by ESA as part of the COLUMBUS contract held by MBB/ERNO. Statements given in this paper should not be construed as official ESA or MBB/ERNO positions.

As the APM is part of a multi-discipline space station maintaining a non-continuous minimum of 10^{-5}G gravity, ESA devised the MTFF allowing for micro-gravity experiments down to 10^{-6}G. APM will be launched by the US Shuttle. The MTFF will be launched by Ariane 5 and serviced by the European space shuttle Hermes. The Polar Platform will be launched by Ariane 5 or Titan IV.

The Polar Platform launch is planned for October 1997. Launches of the APM and the MTFF will take place just before and after the turn of the century, respectively.

The total budget estimate is about $5 billion. According to experience and projection, $1 billion or 20 per cent can be attributed to **software** development and maintenance [1].

2 CHARACTERISTICS OF THE COLUMBUS PROJECT AND SOFTWARE

One of the characteristics of the Columbus project is that it is geographically distributed all over Europe. The expected amount of software is large (several million lines of source code) and the number of people directly involved in software development will be about 500, spread over about twenty different sites.

The software will cover various areas such as on-board automation tasks and various scientific support tasks, crew support, communication to ground support, crew training, system simulation, payload control centres, and mission control centres.

The software will be put together over a relatively short time span (three to four years) and is required to be maintainable over a thirty year period. Consequently, there is the classical need to:

- enforce standardization;
- control development costs;
- ensure quality;
- ease the production process as enforced by the standard.

A software development environment is part of an answer to this need. It is well recognized that automation of a given process as well as tool support for specific methods is of little value to organizations without a controlled and understood process, indeed it can even be counter productive [2,3]. Specifically, it is also recognized that organizations that already have some process and methodologies defined will find it hard, although necessary, to redefine their process in order to satisfy cost and quality requirements for major development projects. This is particularly true for space contractors [4].

3 CSDE FEATURES AND REQUIREMENTS

Thus the Columbus Software Development Environment (CSDE) satisfies the above mentioned needs by offering the software developer an integrated set of tools that will:

- enforce proper use of the methods and notations selected by ESA for use in the Columbus and other ESA software projects: this instantiation [3] of the ESA S/W development standard [4] includes requirements for methodologies such as SADT/ IDEF0, HOOD and languages such as Ada;
- improve manageability, visibility, and communication;
- improve quality and maintainability of large-scale systems;
- facilitate the production of deliverables as required by the Columbus standard (designs, code, user manuals, etc.).

4 CSDE ARCHITECTURAL DESIGN

Two groups of design criteria have been identified for the CSDE. One group can be characterized as the result of external requirements such as support of the ESA standard and maintainability over a thirty year period. The other group is dictated by the choice to support an object-oriented development process model.

The next two sections focus on the most important design criteria followed by a brief discussion of the general architecture.

4.1 External design criteria

The most important external criterion is maintainability as the CSDE should support software development over a period which could well be up to thirty years. It has therefore been of extreme importance to ensure that the CSDE is as invulnerable to changes in the tool baseline as possible. This means that the CSDE to a large extent must support hardware as well as software replaceability.

Hardware replaceability is ensured partly by choice of a secondary platform supporting the same tools, but more importantly through use of a number of standards such as X11 for the window system and X25 for communications.

Ensuring software replaceability is somewhat harder. The software components that make up an environment like the CSDE can roughly be split into three categories, integration platform, tools, and adaptation code. Replacing a tool normally involves making changes to, or even rewriting, some of the related adaptation code. The design of the CSDE makes a point of being as independent of specific tool selections as possible. This is achieved through the use of a data interchange format known as SDIF [10], use of widely applicable methods with well-defined interfaces, e.g. HOOD, and standardized programmings languages, i.e. Ada and ANSI C.

Also as an overall design criterion it should be re-emphasized that the CSDE itself is designed according to the ESA standards.

4.2 Object-oriented design

The most visible feature of the CSDE design is the adoption of an object-oriented principle [9] applicable to both internal design and external appearance of the CSDE.

The reason for choosing this design principle is that it has been found to ensure usability of the CSDE by ensuring a uniform user perception of all areas in the SDE. For example, all data contained in the SDE are in principle represented by visual objects.

Object-oriented design also facilitates maintainability and flexibility as the CSDE evolves over time. It should be noted that the CSDE is designed using a Hierarchical Object-Oriented Design method (HOOD) and contains about 250 objects.

4.2.1 Objects and operations

Traditionally, all data in an object-oriented design are viewed as **objects**. Objects have associated **operations** and attributes. The operations are often referred to as **methods**. Two or more objects may have associated operations of identical names, but with different behavior depending on the nature of the object. Such operations are said to be **overloaded**.

It is a fundamental criterion in the CSDE that all data be perceived as objects. This is independent of the physical realization of the data, e.g. whether they reside in one storage medium or another. All objects share associated operations (methods) and attributes. The operations will obviously differ from object to object, but all objects of a given type have identical operations associated. Depending on the state of the object or, for example, the user accessing the object, operations may be either enabled or disabled, but they nevertheless exist. The same can be said for the attributes associated with an object, some of these may be disabled depending on the state of the object. Operations on an object will be perceived as **polymorphic**; all objects will, for example, have associated a set of **virtual operations** such as open, view, create etc.

4.2.2 Encapsulation

Objects can include sub-objects and are said to **encapsulate** their sub-objects if the operations offered by the sub-objects are made available only through operations on the parent object, i.e. the visibility of operations on the sub-objects is controlled at the parent-object level.

CSDE allows external operations offered by sub-objects only to be invoked after opening of the parent object. Operations which are used internally and hence cannot be invoked by users are identified separately from the user-invocable operations. This design has been chosen in order not to complicate the end-user's perception of the environment.

Figure 8.2 in **4.3.2** below shows a parent object (project: Charlotte's test) with six child objects. One of them (Specification version 1) is open and five child objects are shown. Operations on one of these (Interface Control Document version 1) are shown.

4.2.3 Inheritance

The type of an object may sometimes be refined from another object type, in which case the methods and attributes of the parent-object type are said to be **inherited** by the inferred object type.

The CSDE type hierarchy appears as fairly flat with only one parent-object type. All objects are thus refinements of a generic object type identifying all standard operations and attributes of a CSDE object. Most objects will still offer the standard operations and have the standard set of attributes associated with them. In addition, they may then offer other type specific operations and have extra attributes attached. The reason for this choice of flat hierarchy is that CSDE objects are in general specialized within their own scope. The actual implementation is somewhat more complex and based on refinements of a rather elaborate class hierarchy not directly visible to the user.

4.3 Integration level

The CSDE can be described in terms of the ECMA reference model for CASE frameworks [8] (Figure 8.1), where tools are said to be **integrated** into the CASE environment framework via the tool slots.

An integration of a tool into a Software Development Environment involves three different, but somewhat overlapping, integration aspects [8]:

- data integration – managing the tool's data and data sharing among tools;
- control integration – invoking the correct tool at the correct time and in the correct way;
- presentation integration – integrating the user interface of the tool with that of the environment and the other tools.

An integration is often described as being more or less **tight** (or **loose**). A loose integration is sometimes also called an **encapsulation**.

A tight integration involves a full resolution of the different data entities used in/by a tool. This often implies that a tight integration can only be achieved in cases where all integrated tools use a common data structure. Also, a tight integration implies full control of the work-flow control as well as some process automation. Some level of unification of the Man-Machine Interface (MMI) of the different tools is also desirable (presentation integration).

In an encapsulation this tightness has not been obtained, hence the data structures are unique to the individual tools and the granularity of the data is coarse, meaning that, typically, only entities which are clearly identifiable at operating-system level are available as objects in the environment. It is also typical that each tool will have retained its MMI and that most value-add concerning control integration is coupled to configuration management.

Usually as tight an integration as possible is preferable but this is not always achievable. For example, if a tool provides an open architecture a tight integration may be achieved, whereas integration of a third party tool, for which only an executable is available, would most likely only be an encapsulation. On the negative side, a tight integration does however often imply low scope for replaceability, i.e. the tighter the integration of a tool, the harder it is to replace it by another offering similar functionality. These factors have some influence on the generality and portability of the CSDE as discussed below.

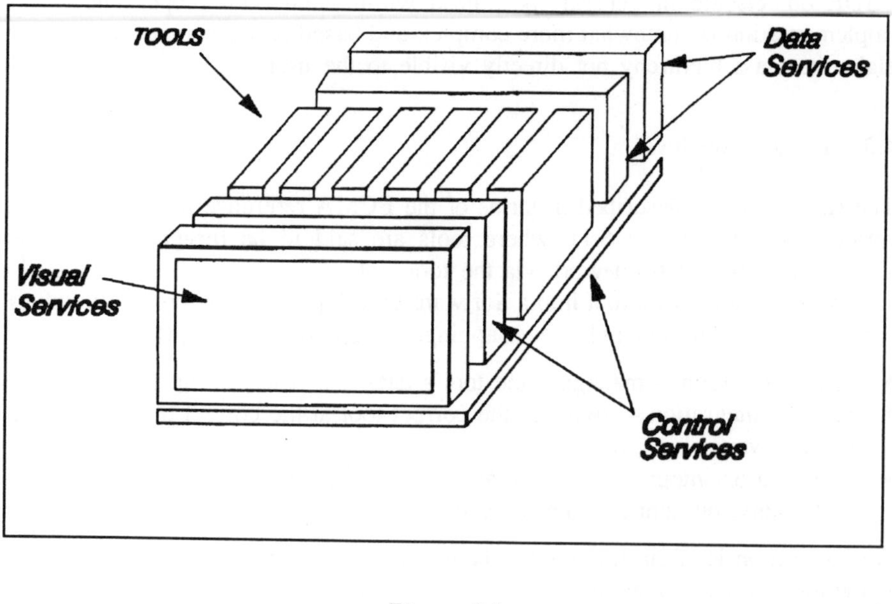

Figure 8.1

Within the CSDE the word integration means data and control integration, sometimes limited to simple encapsulation. Integration does therefore not reflect an attempt to unify the appearance of the individual tools, i.e. their use of scroll bars, error messages, help messages etc. The exclusion of these issues does not imply that they are not recognized as important issues, but merely that their insurance is unobtainable due to the fact that source code modification is not normally an option.

4.3.1 Data integration

A tight data integration is advantageous because ideally it will make it possible for tools to share data. As an example, suppose the HOOD tool managed the object definitions in ASCII format. This would mean that the tool supporting the coding phase, which is the next activity in the life cycle, for example, a syntax sensitive editor, could be directly invoked on these data (or an extract) for further detailing and development.

If a given tool has its own data format, this kind of integration is usually not feasible. Sometimes the integration can, however, be made to appear that way. This is done via interchange formats. Within the CSDE such a format has been defined, the **SDIF** format [10]. It is used for the exchange of data between a number of tools, an example being the interface between the documentation tool (Interleaf 5) and the traceability tool (***Life****LINK by CRI).

In most cases data integration is difficult if the integration is of third party tools only. Only in the cases where the data are saved in a standardized format with a public semantic description (such as Postscript) will this be possible, as for example in the description above. In other cases compatibility is ensured either by the tool vendors or by use of a common interchange format like the SDIF format. In most cases the first solution is not feasible since it ruins the tool vendor's commitment to upwards compatibility.

In general, the CSDE tools have been chosen with data interchange in mind, therefore the problem has been somewhat defused. But for any future additional tools it may become a more serious issue.

4.3.2 Control integration

Control integration is obtained through the design of the MMI and its reflection of the objects and their interrelationships.

The MMI of the CSDE reflects the object-oriented design. The objects, i.e. the data and operations, are represented as icons in a window representing an opened parent object (Figure 8.2).

The icons have associated information which can be displayed either as the object is opened or by clicking the 'Props' entry on the associated menu. Typical information could be whether or not the object is checked out (in use). The operations on the objects appear as menus attached to the individual objects.

The MMI is a dynamic system that will ensure that the user is guided through the correct path depending on the role and state of the selected project. Only the data (icons) available at this given point in time and context will show up.

4.3.3 Presentation integration

An essential part of the design has been to ensure the uniformity of the framework-specific part, e.g. property sheets, menus, icons, and specific type-dependent editors. One very important aspect in the MMI design, as will also appear in the implementation details below, has been the ability to keep the MMI system and its appearance under tight control. The MMI system design is strongly object oriented and implements a high degree of control and reuse.

But, since the CSDE is heavily based on COTS tools, no attempt has been made to force tools into a particular style. However, the CSDE is OpenLook (soon also Motif) based, and tools that obey the look and feel guideline will automatically match the appearance of the CSDE MMI.

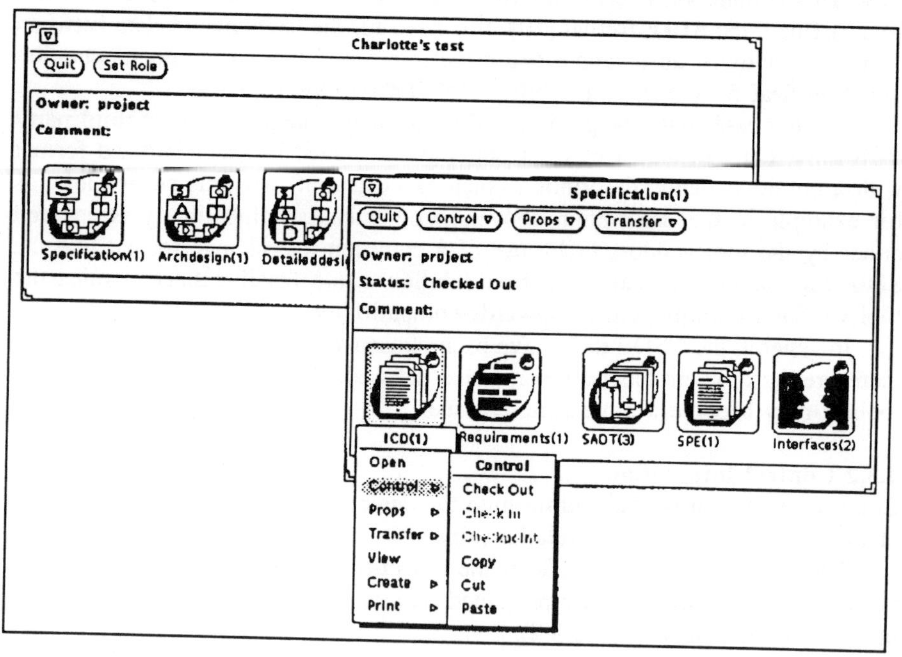

Figure 8.2

4.4 Configurability and flexibility of the SDE

Another important issue to discuss is the configurability of the CSDE. The CSDE has been developed to follow the Columbus S/W Development standards. In most cases these standards clearly define the expected behavior of the CSDE and which functionalities it should offer. However, there is some room for flexibility and configurability. In general the design for CSDE is as flexible as the underlying technology and the selected tools allow. For example, the tables that are being manipulated by the traceability tool are quite generic and can be modified with relative ease. Also, document templates can quite easily be modified.

It is obvious that certain parts of the CSDE would benefit more than others from a high degree of configurability. Staff management is such an example. Staff management includes new user roles, adding and removing users, associating roles with users and attaching users to specific projects. The CSDE is born with a set of roles, but this set may be extended if, for example, a special designated type of user is needed. The facilities for configuration management include such configuration capabilities.

Finally it is important to ensure that the types of data which are to be produced within a given phase of the life cycle are configurable. It could, for instance, be the policy of a CSDE user organization to join the outcome of the architectural and detailed design phases, in which case only one set of data would need to be generated.

4.5 Generality

Generality means independence of specific tools, hence, for an SDE to be fully general, it should be possible to directly replace a specific tool with another related tool offering the same functionality. This is very rarely a possibility, as previously mentioned, and CSDE is no exception.

However, the architectural design of the CSDE is relatively independent of specific tool choices. Tools and data are integrated into an Object Management System (OMS), operations are associated with the objects representing the data produced by the tool. If, however, a tool is to be replaced by another tool offering the same functionality, the task is greatly reduced compared to a totally unintegrated environment which does not make use of the object-oriented view offered by CSDE. The operations offered on the objects are independent of the tool and can be kept reasonably intact. Hence, replacing a tool by another usually requires recoding of the wrapper in order to make the new tool obey the existing interfaces.

4.6 Portability

True portability is only possible for tools and environments adhering to a standard including both hardware platform and operating system. PC DOS and System 370 are such examples. The CSDE is UNIX based and hence only portable with some effort.

However, within the CSDE a certain degree of portability has been ensured by choosing tools that exist in various variants executing on a variety of platforms and conforming with standards for the operating system, the window management etc.

5 IMPLEMENTATION

An SDE architecture like the one described above can be implemented following a number of strategies. In the Columbus project it was decided to base the CSDE development on a phased implementation. Thus, the pre-runner of the current CSDE was based on a very simplistic view, that all the SDE framework should support would be navigating between tools and allowing some data exchange without any real configuration management other than what was already present in the individual tools such as the requirement analysis and traceability tool.

It was decided to implement the current object-oriented CSDE by using object-oriented technology. By this is not necessarily meant object-oriented language support, but rather support for object orientation, with respect to both the development method as well as the repository technology.

One of the main features in an SDE is the capability of supporting **persistent objects**, that is, objects that exist between individual executions of a program, by storing the objects in a database. Normally, object-oriented languages such as C++ do not include that capability, although some of the available class libraries do support some level of persistence. So in order to ensure persistence, one would have to add repository capabilities to the environment, capabilities that would allow not only **data** and **relations** to be stored, but also **methods**. This capability was one of the main requirements to be fulfilled by the chosen framework.

5.1 Framework selection

Software BackPlane (SBP) [7] from Atherton Technology has been selected as the framework on which to build the CSDE.

Several candidates were considered, especially PCTE-based [11] such as Entreprise 2 [12] and EAST [13], both of which were under development, sponsored by the French MoD and ESPRIT, respectively. Both of these environments are built on the same underlying technology, namely Emeraude V12 which is an implementation of PCTE 1.5.

The alternative, SBP, has the advantage relative to PCTE that it allows for object orientation, both with respect to the integration technology as well as its support for persistent object behavior, including the ability to attach and store behavior (i.e. methods) with the objects. It also played a major role; another vendor (Verdix) had based their APSE on the Atherton technology, especially as their Ada compilation system (now SUN Ada) was already selected by the Columbus consortium.

Last but not least, it played a role in the selection process when the French company Thomson, who has a majority in Atherton, announced a migration plan that will make their product ECMA PCTE [14] compatible.

5.2 CSDE type hierarchy, generic object

It was mentioned above that all CSDE types are refinements of one generic type. This is a simplification. The actual implementation benefits from the standard SBP class hierarchy including refinements of some of the base types. The so-called generic type is implemented via an SBP template that is available for each individual tools integrator. The generic type includes a number of operations the CSDE end-user only has indirect benefit from. These operations are there mainly for receiving general messages relating to internal actions such as initializing or querying instance variables. The external operations, on the other hand, are those that the user sees often when operating on the particular objects. These are messages like:

help	pops-up a help window;
edit	opens the data; for example if the object is a HOOD object, the HOOD tool is started on that particular data;
print	invokes the print operation for that particular object;
check-out	checks an object out; this operation is needed before the object can be changed;
check-in	checks an object in; check-in freezes the contents of a checked-out object so that this version can be unambiguously referenced in the future.

etc. .....

The notion of the generic type has been extremely valuable in securing consistency and timeliness in the development process of the CSDE.

5.3 Added framework functionality

The fact that SBP is a procured integration platform and not built especially for the purpose and requirements of the Columbus project implies that some functionality would have to be added. Most of the additions have been externally to the SBP product itself, notably the changes to the standard type hierarchy as mentioned above. Inter-operability between SBP and an RDBMS, as well as a customizable man-machine interface, has been added. This last extension has required an added functionality of the standard product, namely an RPC interface to the command layer of SBP. The RPC interface has since become part of the standard product, allowing SBP to be used purely as an invisible repository server.

5.3.1 RDBMS

A very important part of the CSDE is the ability to handle requirement and interface control traces. By handling is meant the ability, under full version control, to create and manipulate individual requirements, design objects etc., and all related trace information. The CSDE, based on fine-grained information, is capable of automatic generation of trace appendices, requirements chapters, and more.

This kind of information is kept in an RDBMS (e.g. Oracle) that is hidden from the user and is accessed through the integration platform. Consistency throughout the environment is secured by the overall configuration control mechanisms of the CSDE.

5.3.2 MMI

As the design of CSDE calls for an object-oriented user interface, where most, if not all, data (projects, diagrams, users, etc.) objects correspond to an MMI object (icon + attached operations), it was decided not to use the standard graphical interface that comes free of charge with SBP. Instead, a proprietary MMI system was designed and implemented.

The MMI system is dynamic. This means that the CSDE is capable of changing its appearance depending on state, e.g. number and type of child objects of a given parent. The MMI development system is also object oriented in the sense that class libraries are defined for the MMI programmer to use.

The CSDE MMI system consists of:

- an RPC-interface to the SBP server (the client);
- an MMI language (ASL) interpreter;
- and a class hierarchy that implements the actual user interface.

The SBP client is the interface to the SBP. Its function is to pass messages to the SBP and at the same time, via a session protocol, ensure that the MMI keeps control, even while waiting for long repository transactions.

ASL (Application Specific Language) is an object-oriented language developed for the CSDE MMI system. The language is similar to C++, with some Eiffel-like constructs. The language supports all features that are normally expected of an object-oriented language: late binding, inheritance, abstract data types, dynamic creation of instances, and information hiding. ASL includes most of the programming constructs known from C, for example compound statements such as 'if-then-else', 'while', and 'for', as well as many of the operators such as '+', '++', etc.

Like C++, the language does not include I/O either to files or X-windows, but it does support class libraries and function libraries which then include necessary I/O calls.

The available class hierarchy can be divided into four major parts:

- Generic This class defines all behavior common to all object windows. The classes developed by the individual tool integrator, are refinements of this class. Written in ASL.
- Xview These classes constitute the Xview interface. Written in C++.
- Session This class defines all attributes of a session, i.e. the interface functions to SBP. Written in C++.
- Screen These classes define the available window types and their behavior, e.g. icons, buttons, messages, and menus. Modelled in Guide (OpenLook). Written in C++.

The approach taken has the advantage that the individual tools integrator does not need to care about physical design of the system as uniformity is automatically ensured. Another great advantage is the possibility for all members of an integration team to reuse classes refined from the generic class.

6 PROCUREMENT, DEPLOYMENT AND SUPPORT

CSDE consists of a large number of components, most of which are purchased from third party vendors. And a very important part of the system integrator's role is not only to build an integrated environment but to ensure its daily maintenance and operational status. This is not trivial. The technology may be state-of-the-art, the architecture may be optimum, but it is to no avail if it is not deployable.

In order to ensure proper deployment and use of an environment, a number of factors must have been considered and acted upon and a suitable organization must be in place.

It must be secured that each selected vendor is committed to maintain their product(s) over a long period. This is handled by the **contract officer.** The contract officer ensures that a contract exists between the environment provider and each tool vendor. The contract will typically include items such as price/ discount structure, escrow arrangement, and a technical annex describing the responsibilities of both parties. Typically, such an annex will describe any special developments that the vendor has agreed to introduce into the standard product, as well as a compliance matrix matching features against requirements. On the other hand, the contract will also include how the environment provider will execute incoming inspection of products as well as an agreed error and change-handling procedure. The contract should also include schedule information for the environment provider to have at least some form of firm input for his planning.

It shall be emphasized here that central distribution of the environment is mandatory. Even then, the environment provider will not be relieved from customers trying to make their own deals with the vendors, resulting in compatibility and support disasters. The procurement and distribution is performed by the environment provider's **logistics officer**. This person works in close cooperation with the contracts officer and accounting, and is responsible for all procurements and distribution in relation to the environment. For CSDE, the logistics officer is operating under fully commercial conditions, meaning that each individual environment is 'built to order'.

As the environment is built and distributed by the environment provider, it is also natural that support is handled centrally. In the case of large installations one might prefer to have local support representation. Support is the responsibility of the **support manager** and includes training, hot-line, error report handling, and installation support. In the case of the CSDE, the support manager is also responsible for the documentation, the CSDE User Forum, and participates in the CSDE Software Control Board.

7 CSDE STATUS AND FUTURE DIRECTION

CSDE 1.3 has been in active use for about a year with an installed base of about 150 seats. The first version of CSDE 2.0 (as described in this paper) was given to the Columbus prime at the end of 1991. It will be released for general use in May 1992. This version of CSDE will include the following integrated third party tools:

Platforms

- Software BackPlane from Atherton
- Oracle, an RDBMS from Oracle

Cross life-cycle tools

Interleaf 5, a technical publications system from Interleaf

*Life**LINK, a trace tool from CRI

Life-cycle phase tools

ASA, an IDEF0/SADT tool from Verilog

HOOD-SF, an object-oriented design tool from CRI

Key-One, a syntax driven C and Ada editor from LPS

VADS APSE, an Ada Programming Support Environment from Verdix

VADS, an Ada compilation system from Verdix

ANSI C from SUN

The next version will include further tools, especially tools for quality assurance and test.

At the same time as the CSDE is qualified and released, a commercial version, *Life**CYCLE, will be available. *Life**CYCLE is different from CSDE mainly in that each tool integration will be made available as a specific product, known as a tool 'Adapter'. Also, the basic framework including the MMI and ASL will be made available for adaptations to other environments.

REFERENCES

1 McGarry, F. E. et al. (1989) *Ada and Software Management in NASA: Assessment and Recommendations*, NASA GSFC, MD.

2 Humphrey, W. S. (1991) CASE Planning and the Software Process, *J. Syst. Int.*, vol. 1, nos. 3/4 pp. 321-337.

3 Humphrey, W. S. (1989) *Managing the Software Process*, Addison-Wesley, Reading, MA.

4 Langeland-Knudsen, J. and Guldberg, J. (1991) Management in SDE-based Organizations. *Proc. CNES-CGPL* 31, pp. 281-286, Centre Nationale des Etudes Spatiales, Toulouse.

5 *Columbus Software Development Standards*, STD 1213800 000 Issue 4, MBB, Bremen (1990).

6 *ESA Software Engineering Standards*, ESA PSS-05-1 Issue 1, ESA, Paris (1987).

7 Black, E. (1991) ATIS, CIS, PCTE, and Software BackPlane, *Proc. 4th S/W Eng. Conf.*, pp. 601-615, EC2, Paris.

8 *A Reference Model For Frameworks Of Computer-Assisted Software Environments*, ECMA TR/55, Geneva, (1990).

9 Meyer, B. (1988) *Object Oriented Software Construction*, Prentice-Hall.

10 Nielsen, T. B. (1990) *Definition of a Standard SDE Data Interchange Format*, COL-CRI-SDE-TN-0077-90, CRI.

11 *A Basis for a Portable Common Tool Environment*, V1.5, Commission of the European Communities, Brussels (1988).

12 *Atelier Entreprise 2, Guide d'utilisation*, SYSECA, Paris (1991).

13 EAST Environment, SFGL, Paris (1991).

14 *Portable Common Tool Environment (PCTE)*, ECMA Standard 149, Geneva (1990).

9 Open IPSE with Full Life-cycle Traceability

Finn Hass
Computer Resources International A/S

1 INTRODUCTION

The CRI IPSE (Integrated Programming Support Environment) supports the full software engineering life-cycle with the bridge to the system aspects in the requirements phase and the integration, test, verification and acceptance phases.

Emphasis is put on engineering activities, i.e. a general framework is provided for the integration of tools supporting requirements analysis, design, coding, testing, etc.

The IPSE supports invocation of tools on the right data in a generic manner which hides the actual tools and which guides and controls the user access to tools, functions and data as dependant on user-assigned rights. The formatting of data constituents is supported by the framework and the tools.

The IPSE framework contains services – the engineering database – for the storage and retrieval of programs and data. These services encompas configuration management, including data-flow traceability between life-cycle phases, both for large-grain data (documents) and small-grain data (single requirements, design objects, etc.).

The engineering database will contain all the data and the status of data which are required for project management and quality assurance activities.

This brief description of the CRI IPSE will first introduce the major characteristics in section 2. A further, more detailed, description of the CRI IPSE specialties will be presented in section 3.

2 CRI IPSE MAJOR CHARACTERISTICS

2.1 The unpopulated IPSE

The CRI IPSE provides full life-cycle support – upper and lower CASE – for the development of software programs as part of a system. Generic services, however, are available which allow addition and replacement of tools in order to support other languages and methods.

The CRI IPSE offers a basic set of services – life-cycle phase and method independent, but configurable – for the uniform access to, control of, and invocation of operations on **data objects.**

These services define the UNPOPULATED IPSE and incorporate:

- object-oriented man machine interface (MMI);
- object-oriented process management of MMI initiated operations on data objects, thereby implementing a sophisticated data-flow and work-flow management through the life cycle. This includes invocation of external point tools and services;
- repository support with built-in configuration management supplying multilevel, hierarchical registration and version control of both large grain and small grain data constituents(see Figure 9.1).

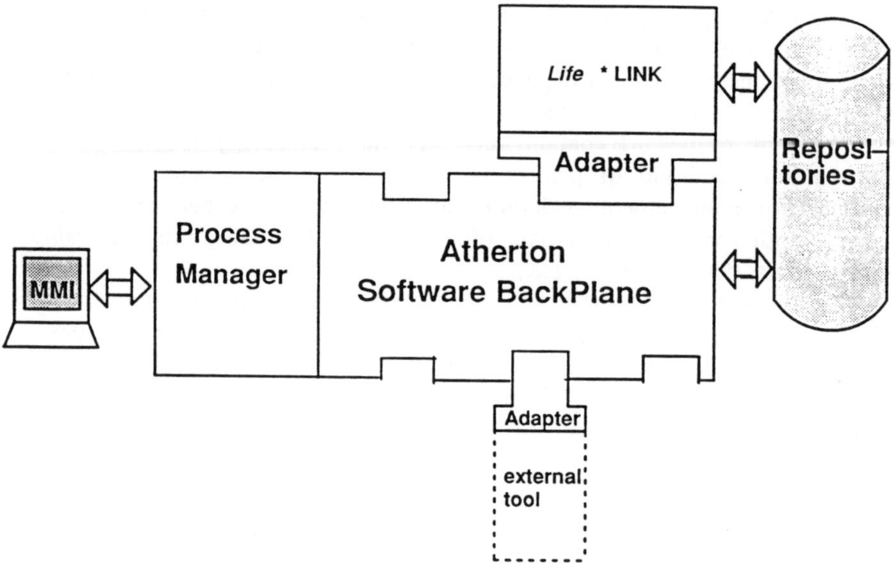

Figure 9.1 The unpopulated CRI IPSE

2.2 Object-oriented man–machine interface and process management

The CRI IPSE presents to the user an object-oriented, strongly iconised and compact user interface. At the highest level of the hierarchical presentation the user sees the iconised system work areas, the formal configuration management area (for released and baselined development data), plus the development project library. The user may navigate further on through selection of a development project icon, whereafter all life-cycle phases are shown as icons. At the next level of a selected life-cycle phase, easily recognizable icons will display the set of data and documentation objects (constituents) to be prepared (see Figure 9.2).

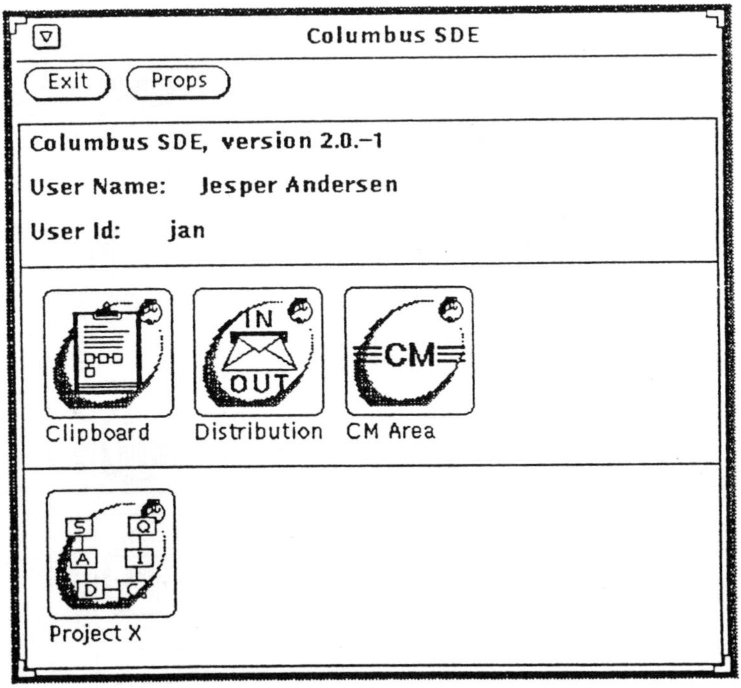

Figure 9.2a CRI IPSE MMI: user entry

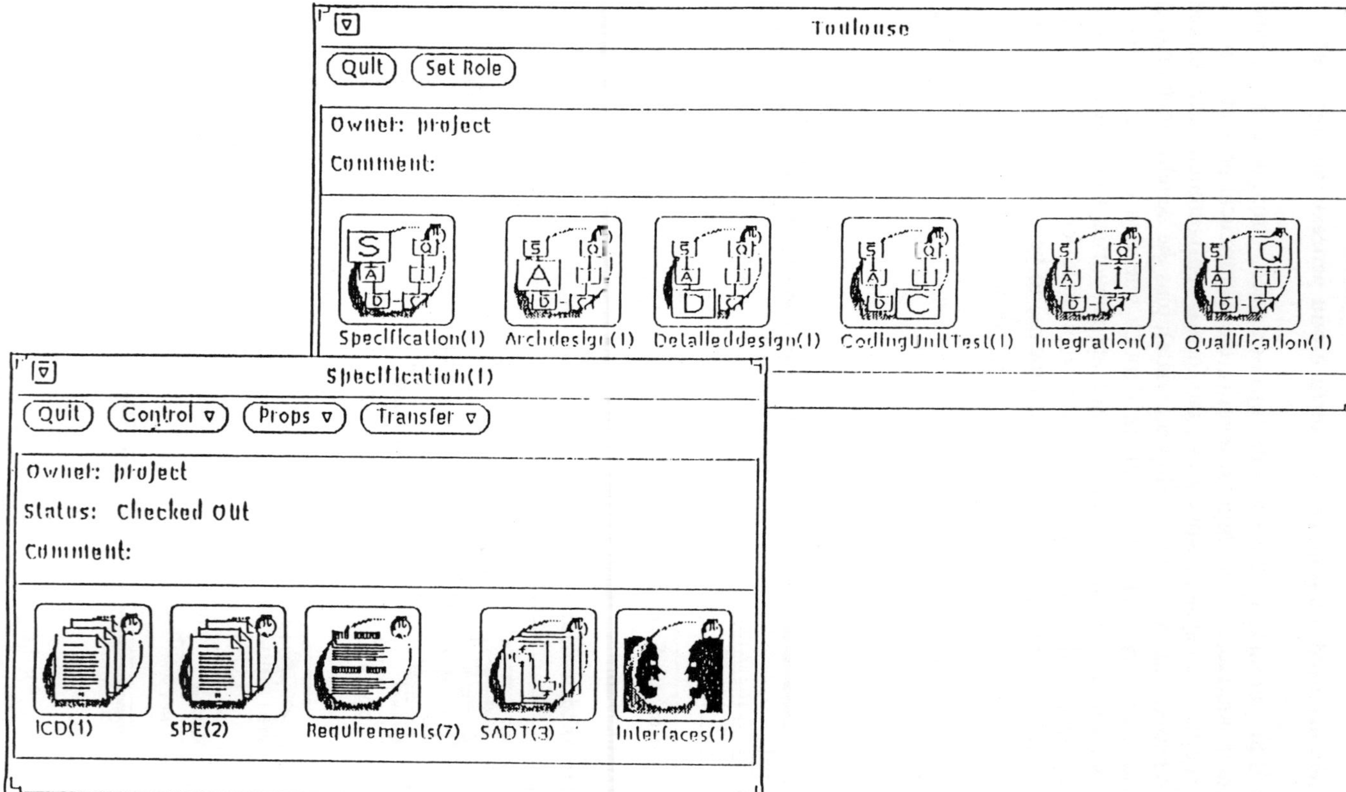

Figure 9.2b CRI IPSE MMI: project and life-cycle phases

Through this well-ordered display the user is guided through the development. Further guidance and constraints are added through assignment to object attributes such as user-dependant roles and access rights, and object status (check-out, dependency on other objects through use links, etc.).

A series of standard (class-object defined) and object-specific operations are available for setting object attributes and invoking external actions on objects.

The operation edit will automatically invoke an external point tool or service (delivered by customer, CRI or third party vendor).

Other operations will initiate the automatic documentation generation from data constituents as based on the use of documentation templates.

Despite the compactness of the user interface, it is highly configurable as it is based on the one-to-one relationship between the objects of a class-object hierarchy of the MMI and the objects of a (CRI-extended) class-object hierarchy of the **Atherton BackPlane**. All object **attributes** (i.e. processing data), **messages** (i.e. operations), and associated **methods** (i.e. processing descriptions) are stored in, or referenced from, the Atherton BackPlane object storage. Whenever an operation is selected for an object in the MMI it is executed through call to the Atherton BackPlane which then, based on object instantiation, will perform the **process management**.

2.3 The populated IPSE

Integration of external tools and services to the CRI IPSE Services is performed through the operations of the process management which will initiate calls via the operating system (e.g. start of process, UNIX RPC, shell script, etc.).

It is thus seen that external point tools and also external services, such as external repositories, may be integrated without changing these. The depth of integration to the MMI and process management (and thus the degree of communication between tools and services) will depend on the openness of the external tools for access to their subfunctionality and internal data.

2.4 Configuration management, use links and traceability

All application configuration management (during development and for deliveries) is controlled, but not exclusively, by the Atherton BackPlane object storage.

Important configuration management measures, in addition to the object hierarchy and version control, are two additional means:

- Use Links for large-grain data consistency and
- Traceability for small-grain data consistency.

Use links facilitates the dependency registration, i.e. used by, between specific versions of life-cycle data constituents of the same and different life-cycle phases. This provides for linking together consistent data constituents without the highly impractical method of changing version numbering for higher-level objects whenever changes occur. It supports the registration of a consistent data set for development and delivery, and it prevents cyclic version inconsistencies whenever two constituents are linked, directly and indirectly, in more than one way. Use links thus supports work flow during development (see Figure 9.3).

Whereas normal configuration management, including use links, is concerned with control of large-grain data objects, such as complete sets of requirements and complete designs, the CRI IPSE also provides a unique, life-cycle-phase independent facility for controlling versions of, and links between, small-grain constituents such as single requirements and single-design objects, etc. – the *Life**LINK function.

*Life**LINK supports traceability, but it also provides a **document database.** Complete document structures or parts of document structures may be stored in the *Life**LINK database which provides full configuration management with version control for formal documents and single constituents of documents. Autonumbering and unique identification is given to single constituents. There is a provision for automatic input from, and output to, the front-end documentation tool. Single constituents of *Life**LINK may be text or graphics in ASCII (see Figure 9.4)

The highly configurable facilities of *Life**LINK for adding attributes to data – not only different types of trace links, but also identification of author or other responsible, the qualification through comments, the identification of editing facility to be used, etc. – make it very valuable as a query facility.

Trace links are established whenever life-cycle methods do not provide automatic consistency (such as for automatic code template extraction from design). Trace links are thus established manually but very easily by pointing out, using the mouse, the constituents actually to be linked from the display of two sets of constituents.

Whereas single requirements and single-test procedures usually are stored physically in *Life**LINK, the design objects and operations may be inserted as names (pointers) only, the description being **physically** in a file in the Atherton BackPlane repository (refer to the Dual Repository description below).

*Life**LINK is highly configurable to different document standards.

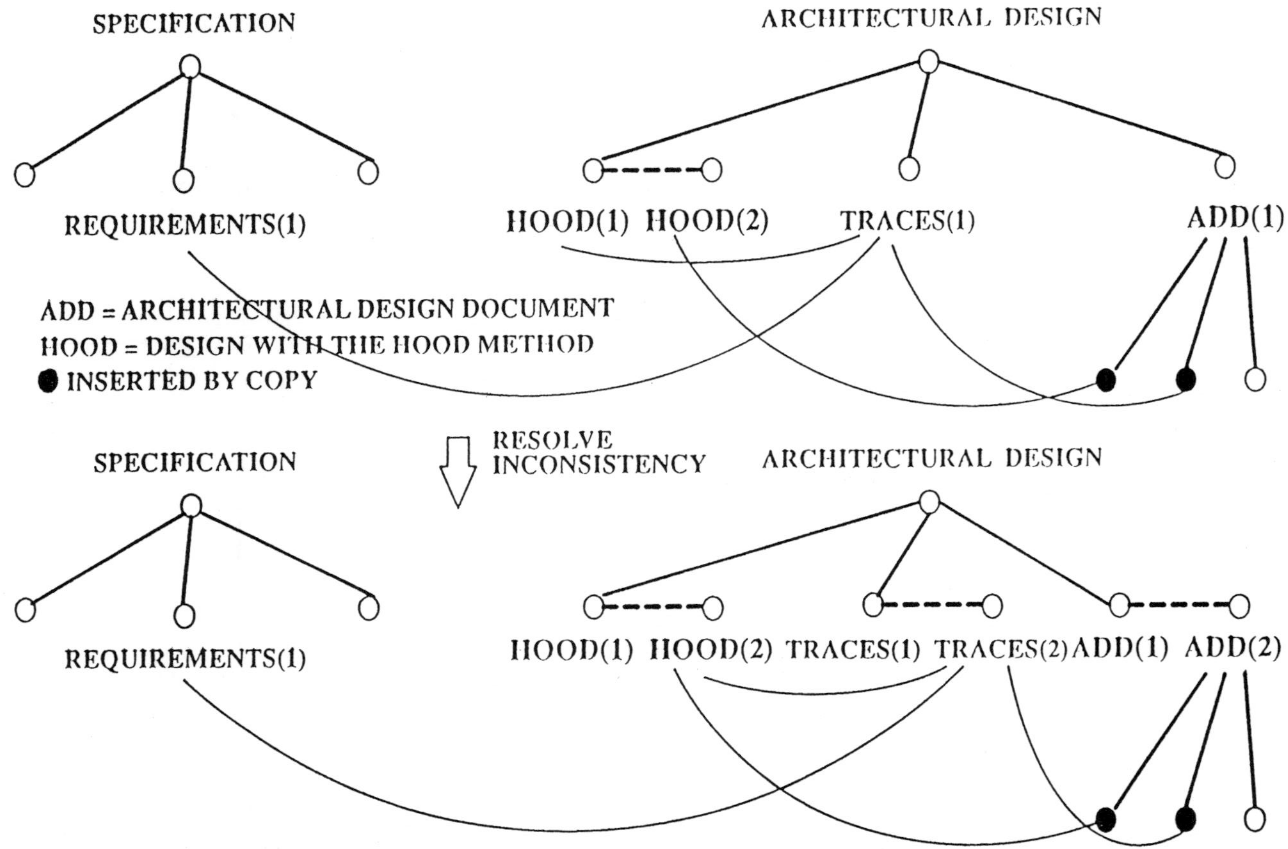

Figure 9.3 CRI IPSE: use links concept

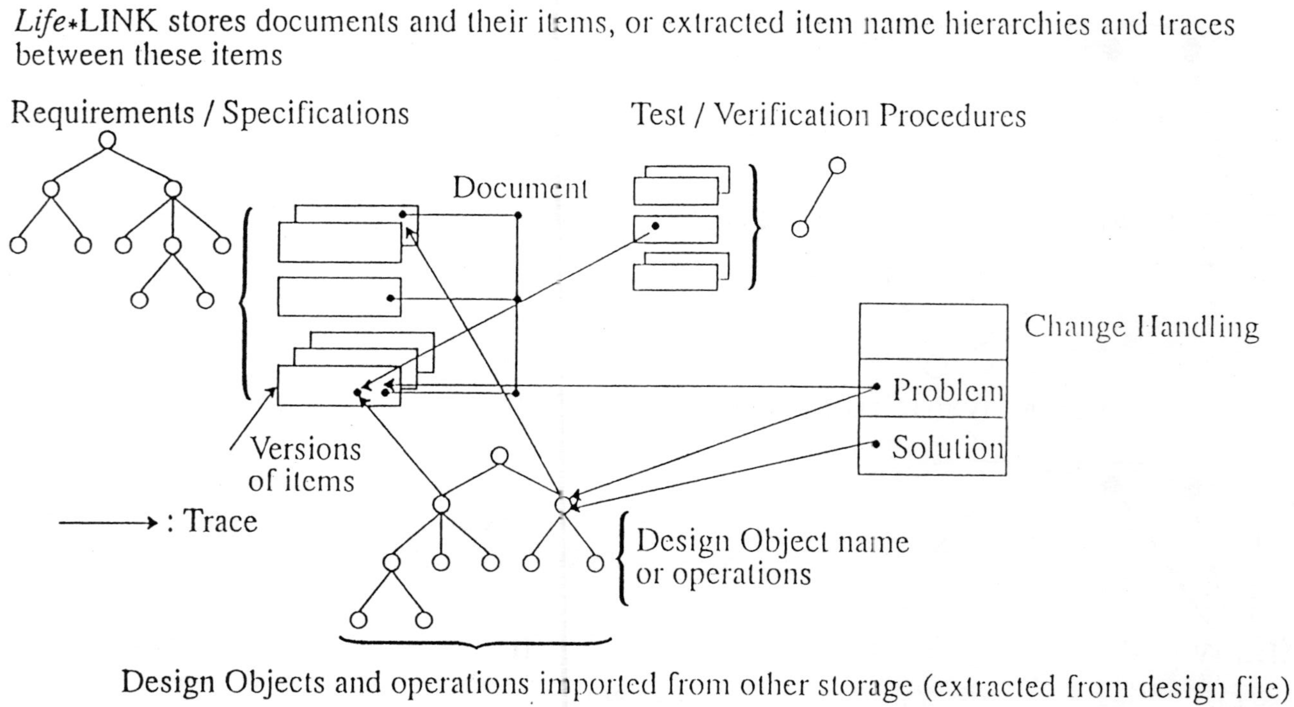

Figure 9.4 CRI IPSE: traceability concept

2.5 Dual repository

The Dual Repository concept is a unique implementational feature of the CRI IPSE:

- The Atherton BackPlane, which is an Object Management System (OMS), provides the major repository, responsible for the central configuration management and all large-grain data control. Data constituents stored elsewhere are referenced via logical objects.
- The *Life**LINK, which is an application based on a Relational Database Management System (RDBMS), is dedicated to the storage and control of small-grain constituents and their trace links to other constituents (see Figure 9.5).

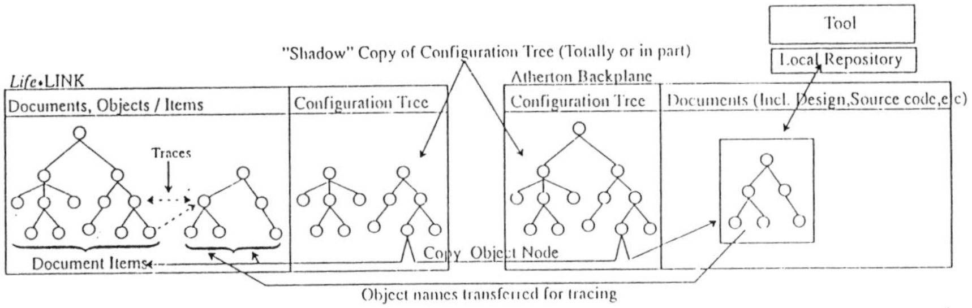

Figure 9.5 CRI IPSE: dual repository concept

2.6 Availability

The CRI IPSE is UNIX based.

It is available with an OpenLook MMI, but is partly available with MOTIF for which final porting is planned.

It is highly portable between UNIX platforms and to hybrid networks of different UNIX platforms.

Presently it is available on SUN Sparc and IBM RS6000.

Access to the repositories is also possible from character mode terminals.

The RDBMS part of the repository, *Life**LINK, is also available on all the most well-known RDBMSs (ORACLE, SYBASE, INGRESS, etc.).

*Life**LINK may also be accessed from PCs and OS/2s.

The CRI IPSE is delivered to the ESA COLUMBUS project and in part to the HERMES project (*Life**LINK).

As a consequence the CRI IPSE is available with an implementation of the ESA standards for software development as a default.

Presently, the CRI IPSE supports Ada programming.

3 CRI IPSE SPECIALTIES

3.1 A highly standardized and configurable mmi and process management system prepared for integration

Use of class-object hierarchies in object-oriented programming provides the basis, once the classes are established, for the easy addition of yet another class object in the hierarchy which will inherit all the properties of the class objects above. Thus object-oriented programming provides for a high degree of standardization and maintainability through reuse, but at the same time supports high flexibility.

In the CRI IPSE, the common MMI and all process management resulting from the related user interaction is built on object-oriented programming and processing. This includes the interface to external point tools and services and their interface to the central repository, i.e. the Atherton BackPlane.

Instantiation of the MMI (see Figure 9.2) is achieved through:

- instantiation of MMI object layout via the MMI class-object hierarchy;
- instantiation of the object data processing via the one-to-one reference between class objects of the MMI and class objects of the process management object-class hierarchy of the Atherton BackPlane, whereby the process management object is instantiated from the object repository of the Atherton BackPlane.

Opening an object (icon) for display of the next level objects (icons) automatically loads to memory the relevant objects, their appearance on the screen, their operations and attributes.

The operations of the MMI (directly visible and selectable or through pull down and pop-up menus), which are a set of class-object standard operations plus object-dedicated operations, are executed through invocation of operations on the underlaying data objects corresponding to the ones selectable on the screen.

Objects are characterized through three sets of parameters:

- attributes (which include the actual data);
- operations (also called messages);
- methods associated to the individual operations.

Methods are actually C-programs, activated on call of the associated operation. The result may be direct change of object attributes or calls to other objects including external tools, for change of data.

As soon as an operation is initiated from the MMI an RPC is sent to the Atherton BackPlane front-end on the local workstation. In the cases of updates or retrieval of information not available locally (e.g. at instantiation), this is followed by a call to the server, where the Atherton BackPlane back-end and repository is located, .

To give an idea of the attributes available for objects, a list of the attributes for the data and documentation constituents under the life-cycle phases given here:

- Data – this part is dependent on the constituent type a SADT object will have a SADT/IDEF0 model associated a requirements object will contain (textual) requirements a project object will have references to a number of life-cycle phase objects, etc.
- Use links. This list contains a reference to each of the constituents used by this constituent.
- Property sheet
  - creator
  - creation time
  - check-in and check-out time
  - version identification
  - type
  - status field – indicates whether the constituent is checked in, checked out, opened or closed whether the constituent is under development, released, or baselined
  - access rights
- Reports. Contains consistency report, completeness report, debug report, link report and similar reports.

3.2 Projects, user roles and access rights

The Configuration Manager is in charge of creating new projects.

Projects and the associated life-cycle phases may only be accessed by users who have been assigned

- a user role and
- access rights.

The following user roles and access rights may be assigned:

User roles (others may be thought of)

- Project Manager
- System Engineer
- Programmer
- SIVQ Engineer
- Configuration Manager
- System Administrator
- Procurement Manager
- Product Assurance Engineer

Access rights

- Read. This access right gives the user permission to apply operations which do not modify the constituent version, e.g. viewing, compilation, printing, etc.
- Write. Permits the user to check out the constituent version and later to check in the modified version. All parts of the constituent version may be changed: data, use list, etc.
- Delete. Allows the user to purge one or more versions of the constituent. It further allows him to delete the constituent. A deleted object is still in the data bank but in detached mode.
- Access control. Enables the user to grant access rights to other users/roles.
- Check out. Permits the user to check out the constituent version, but prevents him from checking in the modified version. The access right is useful when several users are working together on the same constituent; only one user should be permitted to check in the constituent (the one having write access on the constituent), but all users having write access on some part of the constituent should have check out access on this constituent, allowing them to check-out the constituent they are responsible for without being dependent on the check-out status of the ancestor constituents.
- Append. Permits the user to create new constituents within the constituent version.

At start only the Configuration Manager has access control and thereby the right to grant access rights and user roles to others. Usually user roles are given a set of default access rights. Also it is customary for the Configuration Manager to give the access control to the Project Manager; he may then grant user roles to other users.

At project selection, the users may choose amongst their given roles.

3.3 Configuration management: use links and traceability

A project is described by its life-cycle phases, and these are again implemented by generating the proper data constituents which will be part of the phase documentation. In order to show which constituents belong together we may use the version numbering of the project tree extensively, i.e. to the node level where changes propagate (which means to the phase level for changes pertaining to a phase only, and the project level for changes that propagate across phases, etc.). Since higher-level version changes are only effective if it is checked that a consistent data set is available (and furthermore may become rather unmanageable), we have chosen another means: Use Links.

Refer to Figure 9.3 which shows the effect of a design change. This figure also shows the benefit of making visible to the user the data constituents (Design and Traces in this case) as objects for generation independently of their inclusion in the documentation (the ADD = Architectural Design Documentation in this case).

The use link between the Traces (version 1) and the Design (version 1), between the Traces (version 1) and the Requirements (version 1), between Design (version 2) and the ADD (version 1), and finally between the Traces (version 1) and the ADD (version 1) proves the following:

- Requirements (version 1) are traced **from** the Design (version 1);
- A cyclic inconsistency in use links for Design reveals inconsistent use of Design (version) in the ADD.

As a consequence Traces (version 2) should be linked to Requirements (version 1). Traces may only be established along use links. If there actually was a set of Requirements (version 2) that should be traced to, then the link should be moved and a traceability impact report will reveal which impact changes between Requirements (version 1) and Requirements (version 2) will have on the Traces **already** established.

3.4 Configuration management implementation: the dual repository with large and small grain data control

The master/slave relationship between the repositories of the Atherton BackPlane (as master) and the *Life**LINK repository (as slave) is established and preserved by copying the node (object) version number from Atherton BackPlane to *Life**LINK, where the breakdown of the constituents is continued with associated version numbering on lower levels. (see Figure 9.5)

Due to the more advanced query facilities of *Life**LINK, as based on a RDBMS, it is found suitable as a medium for establishing traces between the low-level constituents. Refer to the next section.

3.5 *Life**Link: the document database with built-in configuration management and traceability

*Life**LINK is a complete database for storage and control of formal documents, including items of text or graphics in ASCII.

Formal document means a document which is based on customer predefined templates for its layout and structure of single items. There is a high degree of freedom for structure definition, since *Life**LINK may store any length of free text or graphics in ASCII.

*Life**LINK has complete configuration management support, offering variant and version control on document level. Not only documents but each single formal item (requirement, test procedure, etc.) will automatically be version controlled. Items are automatically numbered in two ways: uniquely, and with a sequential number depending on their position in a section.

*Life**LINK, furthermore, offers multiproject control of documents and the hierarchical relationships between documents, including the possibility of using the same document in more than one project.

It may store the complete document structure with the facility for hierarchical or sequential browsing through the document.

*Life**LINK offers a standardized interface to a documentation front-end, presently TPS/Interleaf and FrameMaker. It is thus possible to enter formal documents prepared with an external editor automatically to *Life**LINK, to regenerate the document in total or part, to edit it again, and re-enter the document to *Life**LINK.

*Life**LINK offers the facility to add customer-defined attributes (author, dates, comments, etc.) to each of the small-grain items of the document as a basis for queries and reports. A special attribute may be available for automatic invocation of an external editor in the case of item selection. *Life**LINK has its own internal editor for correction of text. This editor may be used to edit those attributes not visible at document generation.

Items may be attributed for TRACEABILITY, which basically means a typed reference to another item which is either stored in the same document or in an external document. Formally, trace links are established between a set of items of one type belonging to a document, and another set belonging to another section of the same document or a separate document. (See Figure 9.4)

A special type of trace link is the copy trace, whereby an item is not only referenced but actually (logically) copied to the position from where it is referenced. This is very useful in producing many variants of documents where editing for major or important parts only is allowed in the original source (e.g. interface control documents, user manuals).

The fact that each single item in a document is version controlled is of utmost importance: it provides for the establishment of difference reports without text and graphics (!) comparison. This includes difference reports between any two versions of a document, and it provides for trace link difference (impact) reports by warning the user of possible invalid trace-links resulting from change between two document versions.

Impact analysis is provided through the **navigation** function allowing the following of (multiple) trace links from item to item, from document to document.

Since the document database and traceability function is available on the same terminal where all the development is taking place, it is an easy task for the developer to enter the trace links (with the click of the mouse).

3.6 Data-flow and work-flow support

Work-flow support means the guidance and control offered and forced upon a user through the life-cycle phases in order to produce the data and document constituents in the right order, with the right content, and in a consistent and complete manner throughout the complete lifecycle.

Data-flow support means automation of data transfer or data referencing between life-cycle constituents of the same life-cycle phase and between different phases.

Figure 9.6 displays the data flow of the COLUMBUS project. Automation is achieved in many ways: When a project is defined skeletons for all the documents are made available, within which they are prepared or generated automatically from the data constituents. Traceability will provide the references between low-level constituents of the phases. There is automatic code skeleton generation.

Use links will, in co-operation with the version control, connect the constituents of the life-cycle phases and secure consistency.

Work-flow control is further obtained through the MMI guidance to the data and documentation icons and the automatic invocation of tools once operations are selected.

In all cases, it has been seen how the facilities already explained earlier are contributing to the data-flow and work-flow control.

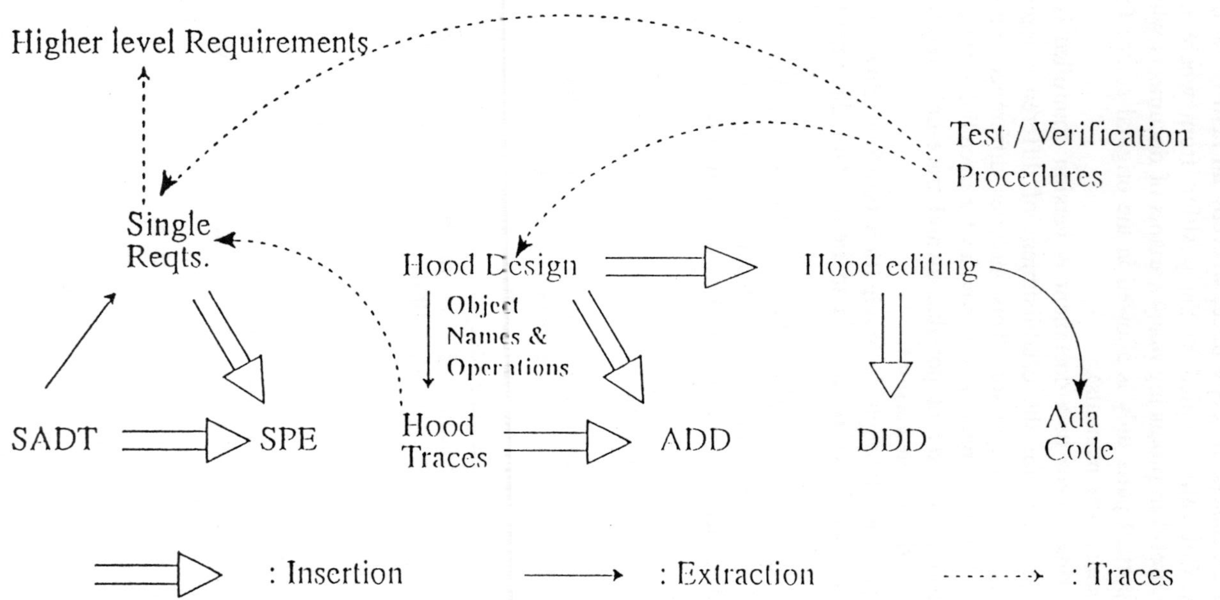

SPE = Specification   ADD = Arch. Design Doc.   DDD = Detailed Design Document

Figure 9.6 CRI IPSE: data-flow and work-flow support

10 Digital's Aerospace and Defence Software Engineering Environment

Paul Bellchambers and Christopher Martin
UK COHESION Marketing, Digital Equipment Corporation

This paper describes the basic elements of Digital's COHESION approach to software development (Digital 1989) and then examines a specific example of the COHESION environment – the Aerospace and Defence Software Engineering Environment.

1 WHAT IS COHESION?

COHESION (Digital 1991) is Digital's approach to open software development. It is built on four fundamental elements:

- architechtural standards;
- support and service;
- integration framework;
- full range of tools from Digital and third parties.

COHESION is both a strategy and a portfolio of products and services from Digital and third party partners.

1.1 Architectural standards

The basis for this is Network Application Support (NAS) which provides a comprehensive set of application services for application access, communication, information and resource sharing. NAS is based on international and industry standards, examples are OSF/1 and OSF/Motif, POSIX, IRDS, PCTE and many more. COHESION is the development environment for NAS.

1.2 Support and service

The most important part of any software development effort is the service and support that can be provided by the vendors of the environment. Digital provides a range of services that support the assessment design and implementation of software development environments.

1.3 Integration framework

Digital's vision of an integration framework is based on a number of levels of integration. These are Presentation, Control and Data Integration.

Presentation integration includes a common user interface and development tools specifically designed to take advantage of the interface. In COHESION DECwindows and OSF/Motif provide the presentation integration.

Control integration is the ability for tools to communicate directly or indirectly with each other and to pass data between the tools in a user-transparent way. The current standard focus for this is the Object Request Broker and Digital's implementation Application Control Architecture Services (ACAS).

Data integration allows tools and applications to share information across the company. The current standard focus for this is the Information Resource Dictionary Standard (IRDS) In Europe the Portable Common Tools Environment is also a major influence on the way tools and data integrate.

1.4 A range of tools

Digital has engineered software for over twenty years and has developed tools to help manage and improve the process of software development. However, third parties are able to provide functionality and tools that fill aspects of the development process where Digital does not have its own tools.

The COHESION environment is designed to support the needs of customers in many different industries who are developing many different types of application – real-time systems, engineering systems or information systems. To support customers in their differing requirements, Digital is taking the broad COHESION product portfolio and building specific application development environments.

The ASD/SEE is the first of these.

2 WHAT IS ASD/SEE?

The COHESION Aerospace and Defence Software Engineering Environment is a customized and extended version of the COHESION Software Development Environment. The COHESION ASD/SEE is tailored to meet the unique software engineering needs of the aerospace defence industry. It is a comprehensive systems solution encompassing not only state-of-the art tools and integration software, but also extensive services.

Digital developed the COHESION ASD/SEE to satisfy an expressed desire of the US Department of Defense for a Commercial Off The Shelf (COTS) software development environment. Digital worked closely with its aerospace and defence customers to ensure their detailed requirements and specifications were addressed. The COHESION ASD/SEE allows customers to support such standards as DoD-STD-2167A – Development, DoD-STD-483A – Configuration Management, and DoD-STD-1815A – documentation of the Ada Programming Language, as well as many other standards. Furthermore, since there are frequently different requirements for customers outside the US, a European Customer Advisory Board has been set up to define a European ASD/SEE.

The COHESION ASD/SEE supports software development roles across the entire software development life cycle. It is designed primarily to support programming-in-the-large, defined to be 500,000 lines of code or greater. From an organizational perspective, programming-in-the-large equates to a department or project development effort involving many small teams. The COHESION ASD/SEE solution will also prove useful for programming-in-the-medium, consisting of 50,000 to 500,000 lines of code.

The COHESION ASD/SEE solution brings together widely used COTS tools from both Digital and its CSOs (Complementary Solution Organizations) into a unified software engineering environment. Through the COHESION ASD/SEE Digital provides customers with a single source for purchase and support of a complete software development environment. As with all of Digital's commercially available products, the COHESION ASD/SEE (including CSO tools, new tools and the integration software) will be supported by a broad range of options from Digital Services. Standard services include user training, and hardware and software support. Customization services are delivered by Digital's Software Engineering Resource Center (SERC) in St. Louis.

Digital is also able to assist customers with the transition from their present software engineering process. Digital is certified to administer the SEI (Software Engineering Institute) assessment; the results of such an assessment could provide a process which would enable software engineering to evolve from an *ad hoc*, labour-intensive activity to a managed, technology-supported discipline.

3 HOW IS THE INTEGRATION ACHIEVED?

In the list of major components there are a number of tools supplied by Digital. Some of these are new and required specifically for the ASD/SEE. These tools are:

- user interface;
- workspace definition;

- interface definition tool;
- component identification tool;
- design communication tool;
- SDF management functions;
- baselining functions;
- metrics management functions.

Let's look at each of these in some more detail.

3.1 User interface

This is an implementation of the DECwindows Fileview utility. It provides a point and click interface with pull-down menus. It provides all the standard Fileview functionality and access to all the ASD/SEE software and it can be customised to suit user needs.

A number of user job functions or roles have been defined as required by DoD-2176A and these have been implemented in the user interface. These roles are based on typical tasks and the associated software required to complete those tasks. Again these are fully customisable via the user interface. The pre-defined user roles are:

- configuration management;
- independent verification and validation;
- programming;
- project management;
- quality engineering;
- software engineering;
- systems engineering ;
- test engineering.

3.2 Workspace definition

A project is a defined set of tasks that require the creation and management of data files. The workspace definition provides the capability to manage data files, for one or more projects, within a defined workspace.

A project is created by providing any valid VMS file name. From this a directory structure is built automatically within the user's default directory with the project name. A VMS logical is also defined so as to provide a pointer to the structure. The directory structure can manage the following items:

- Ada library;
- binary files;
- CMS library;

- DCL command files;
- document files;
- working scratch files.

The Set Project capability uses the VMS logical to set the user context to the appropriate project workspace from the set of defined projects.

4 THE INTERFACE DEFINITION TOOL

This tool automates the definition, tracking and reporting of interfaces between system elements during the life cycle. It supports structured-analysis modelling either as a stand-alone activity of via tools such as Teamwork from Cadre Technologies. The user interface is character-cell based and supports both workstation and non-workstation based users. It is menu-driven for ease of use and there is extensive on-line context sensistive help. Graphics are also supported, enabling objects to be printed.

The interface to external structured analysis tools, which is also character-cell based, enables the user to browse the tool database and migrate interface data into the interface definition tool database. This can be done via an interactive or a callable interface.

The interface definition tool stores interface, signal, physical, logical, systems design and analysis data in a Rdb/VMS database. The data is optimised and held securely. The data can be imported or exported via DCL or from within the tool interactively. The export function allows parts of the database to be baselined. The import feature enables previously exported data to be retrieved. These capabilities support the distribution of the interface definintion databases across organisations and/or companies.

The tool generates ASCII file that can be incorporated into standard reports such as the Interface Requirements Specification, and the Interface Control Document. Reports can be generated interactively or through a callable interface.

The interface definition tool also supports the creation and control of versionable items through an interface to the component identification tool. Which interfaces with the PCMS tool from SQL Software.

5 THE COMPONENT IDENTIFICATION TOOL

This tool is part of the configuration management system. It creates and assigns unique Configuration Item Identification Numbers(CIIN) to software and hardware modules, documents, specifications and other items that must be controlled and tracked by the configuration management system. Each CIIN must be unique across a project even where the project is distributed across many geographical sites.

The user interface is character-cell based and supports both workstation and non-workstation based users. It is menu-driven for ease of use and there is extensive on-line context-sensitive help.

One or more CIIN values can be created for either future or immediate use. The CIIN format is user definable. The user can code information into the CIIN values using available sub-fields, or by using sequential values. The CIIN sub-field values can be alphanumeric, integer, constant, list and range. Configuration items can assigned to each CIIN. Information such as the title and description of each configuration item is permanently stored. A record of when used and by whom the CIIN was assigned is also kept.

To ensure that only unique CIIN values are used across a project the tool supports a network-wide database from which all sites can create, define and access CIINs. They also have access to the information about configuration items. The tool integrates with the configuration management component PCMS by automatically creating configuration items in PCMS when they are defined and a CIIN is assigned. The CIIN is the identifier for the configuration item in PCMS.

The tool also integrates with other applications such as the interface defintion tool for documentation.

6 THE DESIGN COMMUNICATIONS TOOL

The tool provides electronic computer conferencing as a means of communication to support the following areas:

- software design process;
- hardware design process;
- interface design process;
- distributed design;
- capture of design history and rationale;
- action item tracking and status reporting.

Underlying the tool is the VAX Notes product which provides most of the required functionality. Permitted personnel are able to follow and participate in the design process regardless of geographic location. Conferences are enabled by the organisation of information into appropriate domains. A base topic and its replies comprise a conversation within the conference. A set of topics, are typically related, comprise a conference and each user maintains a notebook or list of conferences of interest.

The tool supports users by providing team conferencing functions in the form of guidelines and automated pre-defined command procedures. These procedures can extract new conference information on a periodic basis, forward information onto users via the VMS Mail utility. Also action items can be tracked and monitored in a prescribed manner. The command procedures are user tailorable.

7 THE SDF MANAGEMENT FUNCTIONS

The Software Development Folder functions support the storage, retrieval and management of the contents of the folder. The functions use the feature of the Fileview interface and the PCMS product from SQL Software. The functions enable a number of capabilities.

Via the Fileview interface the user can customise functions that allow the creation, reservation, replacement, fetch, update and unreserve of SDF objects. The objects can be specified by object name or by Configuration Item Identification Number and revision number.

Tools can be automatically lauched to edit or view the contents of supported SDF objects using the tool specified by the user when the tool was created. Tools that can be invoked include, Teamwork from Cadre Technologies, DECplan, VAX Notes, DEC LSEDIT, Interleaf and the DECwindows/Motif CDA Viewer.

7.1 The baselining functions

The baselining functions support the baselining of data held under the PCMS configuration control tool. Typically the data will be stored in one of the following storage mechanisms:

- DECplan database;
- Teamwork database;
- Interleaf desktops;
- VAX Notes conferences;
- IDT database.

These functions semi-automate the baselining of the data under PCMS control via batch processing.

8 THE METRIC MANAGEMENT FUNCTIONS

The Metrics functions enable the collection and monitoring of metrics throughout the software development life-cycle. If properly implemented software metrics can provide early and continuous view of the status of the software development effort. The major activities supported include data collection, reporting, analysis and customization.

Metrics data collection is supported via a base metrics database that contains definitions for an initial set of data that addresses the following areas:

- requirements and design;
- software development progress;
- software development personnel;
- software size;
- computer resource allocation;
- process compliance;
- software change notices.

Metrics reporting is supported by a set of standard report formats. These reports can be generated on demand interactively or in a batch mode. All reports can be viewed, printed or saved into a file. They can be generated in a Postscript format compatible for inclusion into Interleaf documents.

The analysis and customisation of data is supported and the user can select and view data that a standard report was based on. Standard report definitions can be used against user-selected metrics data. The user can also define and create report formats, metric tables and modifications to the standard report formats.

The metrics management functions are achieved through the use of DECdecision DECchart and DECquery tools.

9 SUMMARY

The implementation of the ASD/SEE was specifically designed to meet the requirements of the Department of Defense need for a specific and consistent software development environment. Working with the consortium the ASD/SEE was defined including the process and product requirements. The ASD/SEE is a unique environment that is the result of good and working relationships between all the parties involved.

SUMMARY OF THE MAJOR COMPONENTS OF THE COHESION ASD/SEE

Component	Function	Developer
DECwindows FileView Interface	Provides system access; runs on workstations and graphics terminals; presents users with tools tailored to reflect the needs of the roles or roles held by each user; provides procedures that create and support a standardized workspace.	Digital
VAXset and VAX Ada	Provide design and code functions.	Digital
DECplan	Supports project management activities.	Digital
DECdecision	Management decision support functions.	Digital
DECchart	Graphical representation of data.	Digital
DECquery	Data collection and formatting.	Digital
VAX Notes	Provides the design communications functionality and additional procedures are provided to form a design communications tool.	Digital
Design Communication Tool	Provides electronic computer conferencing and recording of decisions. Addresses DoD-STD-2167A development.	Digital
Interface Definition Tool	Automates definition, tracking and reporting of interfaces between system elements throughout the system's life cycle.	Digital
Component Identification Tool	Used to create network-wide identifiers and assign them to configuration items; works in conjunction with PCMS.	Digital
User Interface	Provides a common interface to all COHESION ASD/SEE tools.	Digital
Baselining Functions	Baseline items under PCMS configuration control.	Digital
Software Development Folder	Electronic storage of software objects.	Digital

Metrics Management Functions	Collection, Analysis and reports of metrics data.	Digital
PCMS	Provides and manages configuration management, including change tracking component identification, and system building.	SQL Software
RTM	Provides the requirements traceability functionality.	SQL Software
Teamwork	Performs system design (structured analysis and design activities).	Cadre Technologies
ADAS	Simulation needs; supports the design and analysis of electronic systems.	Cadre Technologies
Interleaf TPS	Provides the documentation with VAX LSE supporting editing needs.	Interleaf, Inc.

REFERENCES

Digital (1989) The Digital Guide to Software Development, Digital Press, Bedford, Massachusetts.

Digital (1991) COHESION Environment for CASE, Digital Equipment Corporation, Maynard, Massachusetts.

DoD-STD-2167A (1988) Defense System Software Development, Department of Defense.

MIL-STD-483A (1985) Configuration Management Practices for Systems, Equipment, Munitions and Computer Software, USAF.

TRADEMARKS

11 Entreprise II: The Software Engineering Integrator

A. Legait
SYSECA, France

1 ENTREPRISE II: THE DEVELOPMENT ENVIRONMENT FOR MAJOR SOFTWARE

Entrepris™ II users are in the technical and scientific software industry and include members of software development and maintenance teams at all levels: administrators, project managers, project leaders, those in charge of sub-projects or tasks, developers and maintenance staff. Entreprise II is also designed for software tool editors, who need an integrated CASE tools environment in which they can develop and distribute their own tools.

Developers of software systems face numerous problems directly related to software development, upkeep and maintenance. Entreprise II provides a solution to these problems, at both organizational and technical levels.

1.1 Controlling the organizational factors

This involves defining, formalizing, implementing and monitoring the development of software applications to be integrated in a system whose installation requires complex structures and the co-operation of specialists from different fields (concurrent engineering).

These activities take place in an industrial environment which is heavily influenced by the following:

- worldwide structure of large organizations;
- need for international co-operation between organizations;
- geographical distribution of development sites;
- difficulty of managing complexity, organization, cost, production and installation deadlines of the projects;
- diversity of projects and capabilities involved in software production;
- diversity of projects undertaken by any organization.

1.2 Controlling technical factors

It is important to control the factors affecting software development quality in the following areas:

- increasing complexity of software applications;
- rapid technological improvement;
- increasing diversification of software applications which results in ever greater demand, and consequently the need to increase the developers' individual and collective productivity;
- extended life of software applications, resulting in the need to prolong the period of software maintenance and to increase investment in maintenance;
- increasingly strict quality requirements due to the introduction of software in the critical parts of sensitive or high-risk systems.

1.3 Controlling the maintenance factors

The increase in maintenance activities is forcing software developers to find ways to automate and support the maintenance tasks. The reluctance of software developers to devote time to these tasks (they generally prefer to focus on development), as well as the lack of qualified software developers to meet development demands, contribute to the growing imbalance between development and maintenance. Large organizations have to look for solutions which improve automation of development and maintenance. Method tools, formalization tools and support tools for software development and maintenance techniques existing today on the market are extremely diverse.

Therefore, the first problem to tackle in the process of automation is this diversity of tools, which can be overcome by modelling and formalizing the organization of the development and maintenance processes.

1.4 CASE tools fragmentation

The current range of CASE tools is characterized by:

- the existence of varying and incompatible basic methodologies;
- numerous differing, incomplete and unrelated methods;
- a disorganized range of tool-type products.

This fragmentation in methods and tools appears to be the most serious factor hindering production and quality control. The level of investment required to obtain a total solution may be one reason for this fragmentation. Each tool supplier tends to limit itself to solving problems relating to a single part of the development process. Thus we find a large number of specification, design, programming and test tools, but a total lack of complete environments.

This situation, in turn, results in fragmented software development practices and often forces developers to perform manual transitions between phases in the software life cycle. For instance, the lack of automation in the transition between the design and coding phases means that developers have to provide documents proving the progression of the design phase and the justification for moving to the coding phase. These documents form links and reference points between phases, which should be available for reuse in maintenance phases or when backtracking from coding to design. These manual procedures generally make the development process inefficient and also complicate the maintenance process.

It is essential to find solutions which enable integration and automation of the entire development process.

1.5 Horizontal and vertical activities

The software development process includes two types of activity:

- life-cycle activities (simulation, prototyping, specification, design, coding and testing);
- cross-life-cycle activities performed during development (project management, configuration management, documentation, quality, reuse, etc.).

In order to integrate the development process we have to define the general frame for these activities and in particular decide which data will be used and by which methods the data will be handled in terms of rules, rights and responsibilities. The automation of the development process calls for the creation of tools which can support both horizontal and vertical activities and transitions between activities.

The facilities and architecture of Entreprise II have been designed to meet these support requirements for the whole range of development and maintenance activities for large software applications. The design stage involved collaboration with a number of major technical French users: Thomson, Aérospatiale, Dassault Aviation, Dassault Electronique, Sextant Avionique, Sagem, Sfim and the Délégation Générale pour l'Armement.

2 ENTREPRISE II, A LAYERED ARCHITECTURE

Entreprise II is based on a layered architecture. The first layer includes the software framework, providing interface facilities with the various tools in the environment and complying with a data communication protocol. The next layer contains facilities for integrate software tools. These facilities can be grouped together under the generic term backplane. The whole system used to integrate CASE tools forms the Integrated Project Support Environment (IPSE). When vertical software engineering tools of various origins are inserted into this open environment, it becomes a Populated Integrated Project Support Environment (PIPSE). The system always uses the same look and feel.

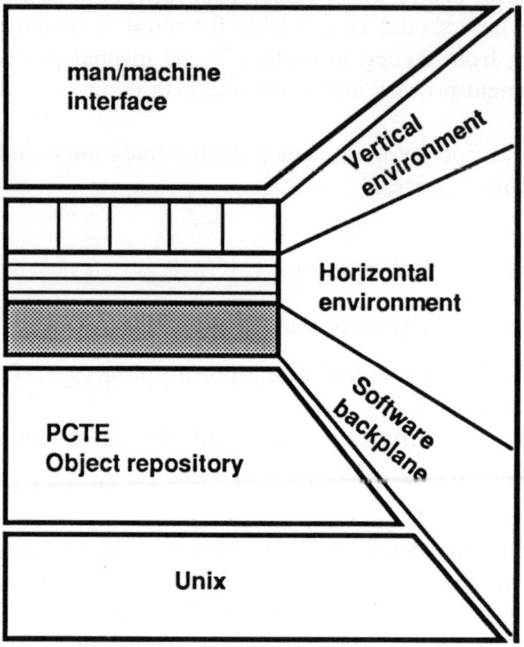

Figure 11.1 An open layered architecture

2.1 PCTE: the Entreprise II software framework

The software framework is the communications channel for all the Entreprise II components. It uses the PCTE 1.5 (Portable Common Tool Environment) standard.

The software framework is a critical element for the interaction of software systems, whether they are development environments or applications developed and maintained using these environments. It is essential that the software framework should act as a standard, guaranteeing long system life and attracting suppliers of tools, environments and applications.

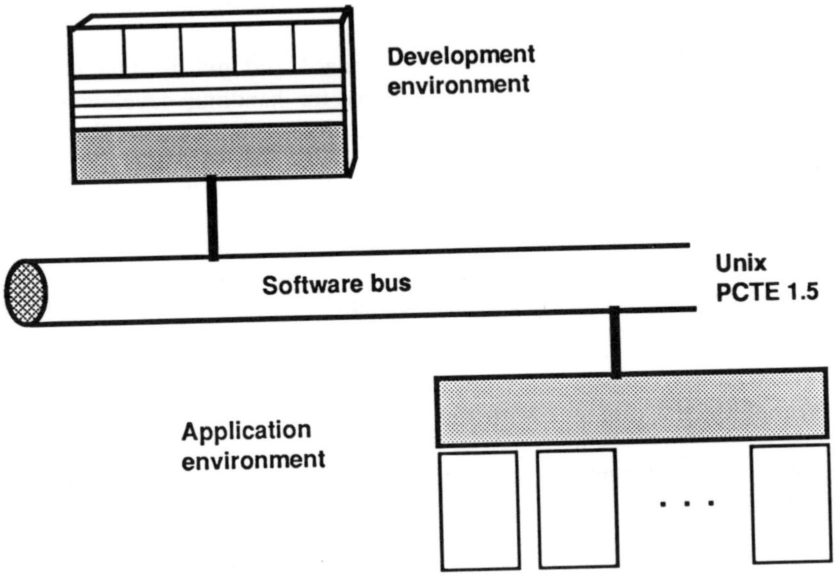

Figure 11.2 The software framework: the key to system interaction

2.2 The software backplane

The software framework alone, whilst essential for an integrated environment, is not the only prerequisite. The homogeneity of the environment's methods and tools requires compliance with a set of principles and rules implemented by the Entreprise II backplane. This backplane is supported by PCTE and makes it possible to formalize the development – maintenance process:

- integration of the organization in the process;
- setting up effective communication between all teams and organizations, particularly to accelerate the decision-making process;
- setting up the means to follow up and inspect the development steps;
- adaptation of the methods and tools used to the specific requirements of the organization, projects and individuals;

- need to integrate a coherent quality control policy which aims to increase the automation of inspections.

All these requirements must be solved within a coherent frame for which foundations must be laid. This is the role of the Entreprise II backplane. Without this backplane methods or tools assembled within an environment would be heterogeneous and incoherent.

PCTE itself defines a number of standard and public data schemas. Entreprise II thereby constructs a philosophy for handling development and maintenance. The Entreprise II schemas define three types of data dictionaries:

- nomenclature-type dictionary covering all data for managing the IPSE and information concerning methods;
- encyclopedia for each project developed in the IPSE, which contains all data produced during development and maintenance;
- reusable objects data dictionary containing all data which can be reused from one project to the next.

2.3 Managing the dialogue with the user

Entreprise II is an interactive development environment. The dialogue is standardized whatever tools are employed by the user.

When the user connects to the workstation, he enters a session, i.e. an environment composed of an IPSE, a project, a task and a role:

- at the project level, Entreprise II defines the tasks on which the user can work;
- at the task level, Entreprise II determines whether the user belongs to the group of users allowed to participate;
- at the role level, Entreprise II determines the tools to which the user has access rights and allows him to customize the presentation of these tools.

These measures contribute to the security of environment functions according to the following basic principle:

> *The only functions presented to a user are those for which he is authorized.*

One user may be connected to various tasks belonging to various projects within a single environment. The user can only activate the tools associated with the task on which he is working.

The command language and the graphic navigator are used to navigate around the data dictionaries and activate the tools (with a display or graphic table for selection of options and start-up parameters). Graphics are used for dialogue with the user. Expert users may alternatively use a text command language for dialogue. The look and feel of the Entreprise II dialogue complies with the Motif™ or Open Look™ standards. The open-ended design of Entreprise II's man/machine interface means that it can be adapted to other look and feel standards.

2.4 Structuring the development

Entreprise II enables its users to base their development structure on four simple, yet powerful concepts:

- the tree (root + nodes) built by the user, which forms the general frame: the participants will look here for the information required and will place the objects they produce in this frame;
- the object sets, positioned on the tree nodes;
- the objects, arranged in sets;
- the relationships: the user or the tools used may establish relations between the three types of entities in accordance with the semantics defined and in compliance with the basic rules imposed by Entreprise II.

These trees, sets, objects and relationships can also be used to define the principles for navigating within the project data base (encyclopedia). The user can add attributes to these entities to facilitate navigation and selection.

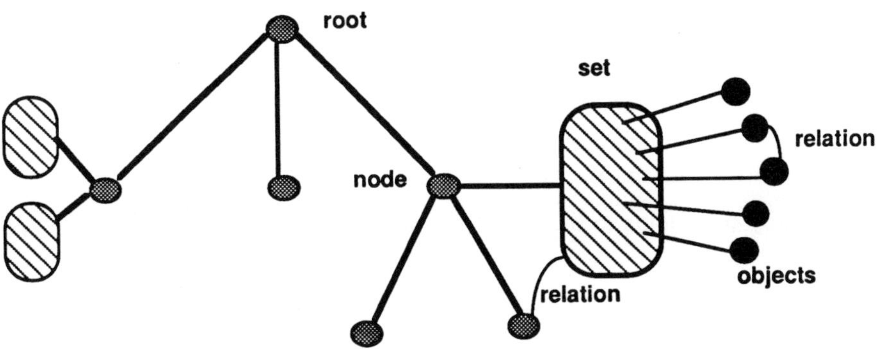

Figure 11.3 Four concepts for a general structure

This structure, defined by the user, is the working basis for all the tools integrated in Entreprise II. Tools must therefore position within this structure all data that can be shared with other tools. This data can be of any type (text, graphics, images, etc.).

This tree-structure is used for project management, document management, configuration management, reusable objects, specification, design, code, etc. The tree concept has enabled the creation of a unique graphic display and navigation system. The system for all the functions of Entreprise II, whether original or added, is independent of the tools and very efficient. The project methodologies are also based on this model. In fact, methods such as DoD 2167A or GAM T17 V2 actually impose a tree-structure organization of developments.

As an example, Entreprise II offers software developers the possibility of building their own structure to conform to the breakdown of the software they have to produce. In this way, the reference tree used by the project reflects the software developed:

- the root of the tree corresponds to the software;
- the breakdown of the software into software elements (and subsequent breakdown of these software elements into other elements or components), results in the development of the complete tree;
- the software objects produced (e.g. specification and design documents, diagrams, code, binary data etc.) are organized into sets and positioned on this tree.

2.5 Controlling data access

The nomenclature database is used to carry out a number of checks concerning data confidentiality. These checks depend on:

- the data schemas, loaded at connection, which define the user's view of the project data dictionaries;
- the tools available to the user during a session;
- the access rights used by the tools to control user action;
- the user's access rights.

This security also helps to increase productivity as it eliminates many types of potential errors.

2.6 Managing the versions

The encyclopedia database associated with each project contains all the objects produced during the project (documentation, sources, binary data, technical notes, etc.). A standard data set is associated with each object in the encyclopedia. Each tool or user can customize its/his view of the objects by defining and adding the data and relations it/he requires. The following basic functions are available to the user for handling trees, sets, and objects:

- editing, for modifying an entity;
- stabilization, for prohibiting modification of selected entities;
- duplication, which allows several users to work simultaneously on the same entities;
- synchronization/delivery, which keeps the user informed of modifications performed on these duplicated entities by other users.

These functions provide coherent version management in all development activities, regardless of the type of objects handled by users.

2.7 Administering the IPSE

Entreprise II is used for administration of the environment, managing security and confidentiality of all the components (methods, tools, participants, products, etc.).

The backplane is the host structure for CASE tools used in the environment. It defines the general frame for the development and maintenance processes, including:

- method: before using Entreprise II, the project leader defines the methodological frame for development, which allows the environment to be configured accordingly; Entreprise II can be used for all standard methods and also allows the project leader to define his own method; the incorporated default methods are GAM-T17 (V2), MIL-STD DoD 2167A and DO 178A;
- organization of the software life cycle;
- company and team practice;
- tools used in the different phases of the software life cycle;
- man/machine interface: Motif or Open Look based on the X.WINDOW™ standard.

3 FEATURES OF ENTREPRISE II IPSE

The Entreprise II integrator development environment supports the facilities which are common to all phases of the software life cycle. The three main productivity factors in major software projects are configuration management, documentation management and project management.

3.1 The Configuration Manager

Configuration management means management of product versions at the development stage (changes), or maintenance stage (evolutions). The Configuration Manager is used to automate the following:

- configuration of all or part of the software (definition of a version);
- generation of a version;
- consultation of a version;
- management and archiving of versions (history, dependency, etc.).

The following four types of standard entity are provided for managing modifications:

- software problems reports sent by end-users of a version; incorporation of modifications to response to these reports can be refused, delayed, or accepted;
- evolution requests intended for the maintenance teams; these requests represent requests for modification that have been accepted;
- change requests attached to a version, which include all modification sheets incorporated during the development of a version;
- modification sheets.

The Configuration Manager can be used for all industrial methods and practices. It allows the user to trigger operations (defined by the user) when the status of these entities changes. It also allows the user to define other types of entities and other statuses or types of transition between statuses.

These customization possibilities, which are vital for incorporating the specific characteristics of each company or project, make the configuration management tool the prized partner of software maintenance teams.

3.2 The Traceability tool

The Tracability tool allows software modules to be followed throughout the different phases of their life cycle. The Tracker provides a horizontal view of software production through the various tools used for specification, design, coding, and tests. It is particularly valuable for tracking software specifications throughout the different stages of development, i.e. for recognizing to which part of the specifications a development object (e.g. design diagram or code part) is related.

3.3 The Documentation Manager

The Documentation Manager automates production and management of the technical documentation relating to a project. Where a certain development method has been associated with a project, a documentation diagram allows the documentation to be automatically structured according to the same method, using the software breakdown tree.

The Documentation Manager automates document production and ensures its coherence, using standard DTP (Desktop publishing) tools. The Documentation Manager tool currently uses TPS™ and/or Framemaker™ tools, as selected by the user. It is an open system, allowing other tools to be integrated as required by the user.

3.4 The Project Manager

The Project Manager tool provides help with all project supervision tasks, using environment data:

- structuring;
- organization;
- estimation;
- planning;
- scheduling;
- follow-up.

The Project Manager is interfaced with the ARTEMIS™ product which may be used as a project management tool for the system featuring the software developed or maintained using Entreprise II.

The integration of ARTEMIS in Entreprise II enables data to be exchanged between the two environments and checked for consistency.

3.5 Code production

Coding activity depends not only on the programming methods but above all on the programming language and the production technology used (editors, compilers, linkers, loaders, symbolic language debugger, library manager, etc). With the Entreprise II production tool, coding activities do not depend on the production technology used, as its programming environment provides coherence between the different tools.

Entreprise II currently integrates various production (compilation) technologies for ADA, C, C++ and LTR3 languages. It provides the programmer with a source organization model which is independent of the programming language used. It gives programmers the means to navigate and graphically display the source texts of code objects. It stores in memory the relationships existing between source objects (at input) and/or binary data (after compilation) for one application. It ensures, if required, consistency between all application objects.

For all programming languages supported, it provides compilation or automatic re-compilation of the application. It automatically creates executable applications. It provides the programmer with a powerful multi-language syntax editor for inputting his source objects free of syntax errors. It manages interdependency of source objects (ADA, C++, C, LTR3, etc.) so that transformations (editions, compilations, etc.) can be applied. These language-specific transformations are defined when a compilation technology is connected to the production tool. It manages the program production environment, e.g. checking the presence of library interfaces for the production of ADA binary data, or that files returned to a C source by **#include** commands are present.

The Entreprise II production tool is an open system, allowing various compilation technologies to be integrated. The list of technologies integrated so far is not exhaustive – other technologies will be integrated to meet the needs of users.

3.6 The Reusable Object Dictionary

Sometimes some objects (source programs, document frames) developed during one project need to be reused for another project and stored in a specific data dictionary. The Reusable Object Dictionary manages objects common to all projects in the environment. Its data are stored using a theme tree. Facilities available are:

- archiving, which allows the recording of objects considered to be reusable,
- consultation of the dictionary, with a search function for selecting reusable objects,
- extraction, which allows the reusable objects selected to be inserted in the current project encyclopedia.

This tool forms the basis for software reuse operations.

3.7 The Communication Manager

Three levels of communication are provided by Entreprise II:

- E-mail between users (software development or maintenance teams) working on the same project or on different projects in the same IPSE;
- composition, broadcasting to lists of users and display of notes, agendas, minutes of meetings, etc.;
- communication of objects between project databases located in remote installations.

This set of tools provides the developer with a real office system environment.

4 FEATURES OF THE PIPSE

Entreprise II covers all phases of a software product's life. It is an environment open to all types of vertical tools and standardizes currently available horizontal tools. There are two methods of integrating CASE tools into the backplane:

- loose integration;
- tight integration.

The backplane has a standard toolkit for loose and tight integration of CASE tools. This allows users to integrate the tools they wish to use in Entreprise II, and enables the horizontal services to be applied to the objects produced using these tools.

The operating dialogue respects either the Open-Look or Motif standard, as required by the user. Entreprise II provides tool integrators with a module to help them design and create these dialogues.

Each tool uses in-built access rights to carry out checks enabling it to adapt its operation to the user's requests and access rights. Entreprise II provides services for developing interactive tool dialogues. Dialogues can thus be created on X.Window which respect the selected look and feel standard.

The Entreprise II backplane thus offers a number of services for developing integrated vertical tools, including:

- a specific user environment;
- a dialogue manager;
- a window manager;
- services providing access to data dictionaries;
- all PCTE facilities;
- an integrated command language (Shell);
- a graphical navigator.

Buying a new development and maintenance package will not mean that previous investments will be wasted, as Entreprise II can host existing tools, making them usable in an Entreprise II workbench without implantation on PCTE. For this, Entreprise II can be used to create host capsules (loose integration). Entreprise II allows data exchange between a project encyclopedia and the host operating system (UNIX™). For example, host system files can be retrieved in an encyclopedia, and encyclopedia objects can be communicated to the host system. These exchange services are particularly useful for hosting tools.

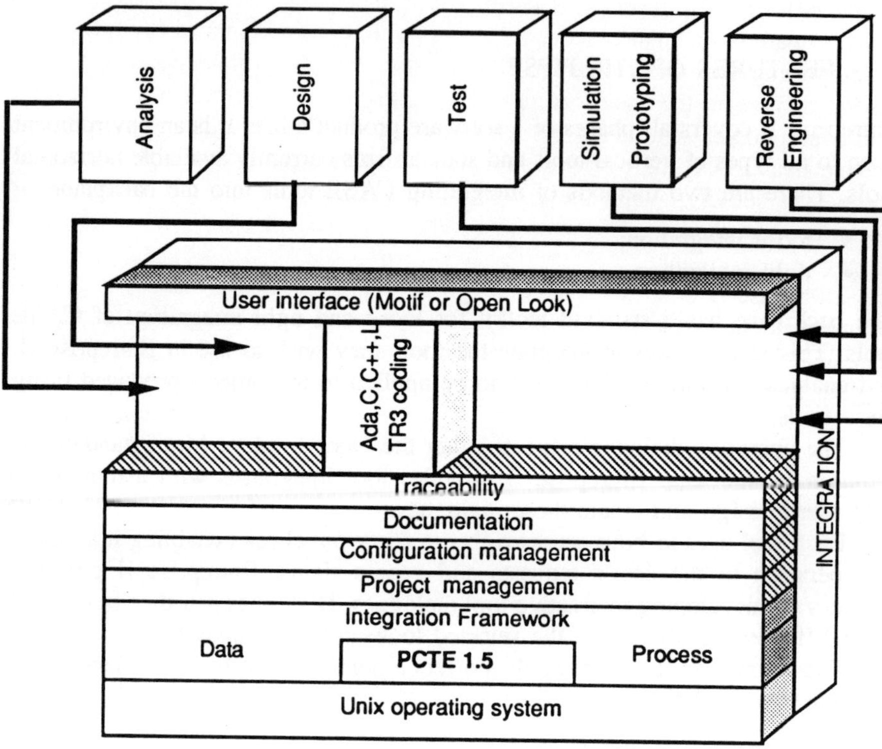

Figure 11.4 Vertical tools in the IPSE

Different software manufacturers use different vertical tools and related methods. To allow for this, Entreprise II can accommodate all vertical tools required by its users, whether these tools are commercially available or owned by the manufacturers themselves. Entreprise II thus provides various tools for simulation, prototyping, specification, design, coding, testing, maintenance, etc. within one project or for different projects in the same IPSE.

5 ENTREPRISE II – AN OPEN INTEGRATOR OF SOFTWARE ENGINEERING SOLUTIONS

Entreprise II is the ideal environment for developing medium- and large-size software applications. It is typically used for projects involving 100 000 or more lines of code, where the standard activities of specification, design, coding and testing account for only 30 per cent of the total cost, the rest being accounted for by project, configuration, documentation and maintenance management.

Software maintenance accounts for more than 50 per cent of the total cost, so integrating horizontal tools used for configuration, documentation and project management with the standard vertical tools used for specification, coding, etc. results in a 30 per cent increase in productivity, starting from the second project. The vertical tools improve the performance of individuals in their particular production activity, while the complete, integrated Entreprise II environment works to meet the goal of increased productivity on a higher level, i.e. that of collective performance.

Entreprise II is an open integrator of CASE solutions. SYSECA is part of an independent partnership, the GIPSY. The aim of this partnership is to unite all CASE tools manufacturers and retailers working together with Entreprise II to give their customers new levels of productivity, security and long product life.

TRADEMARKS

- ARTEMIS; is a registered trademark of Lucas Management Systems
- ENTREPRISE is a registered trademark of the Délégation Générale pour l'Armement
- FRAMEMAKER is a registered trademark of Frame Technology
- MOTIF is a registered trademark of OSF (Open Software Foundation)
- OPEN LOOK is a registered trademark of AT&T
- TPS is a registered trademark of Interleaf
- UNIX is a registered trademark of AT&T
- X.WINDOW is a registered trademark of MIT (Massachusetts Institute of Technology)

Contributors

Jesper Andersen
Computer Resources International A/S

Paul Bellchambers
Digital Equipment Corporation

Eric Black
Atherton Technology

Kathy Chapman
Digital Equipment Corporation

Richard Daley
Richard Daley Associates

Alan J. Gater
Oracle Corporation

Cheryll S. Gerelle
IBEX Computing SA

Finn Hass
Computer Resources International A/S

A. Legait
SYSECA

Henrik Maegaard
Computer Resources International A/S

Christopher Martin
Digital Equipment Corporation

Andrew Mercer
Software One Limited

Ken Thompson
The Institute of Software Engineering